Also by Robert Marro Jr.

Ebenezer Scrooge and the Ghost of Christmas Love

MALACHI MARTIN

In the Shadows of the Vatican

Robert Marro Jr.

POST HILL
PRESS

A POST HILL PRESS BOOK
ISBN: 979-8-88845-670-5
ISBN (eBook): 979-8-88845-671-2

Malachi Martin:
In the Shadows of the Vatican
© 2025 by Robert Marro Jr.
All Rights Reserved

Cover design by Jim Villaflores

Post Hill Press
New York • Nashville
posthillpress.com

Published in the United States of America
2 3 4 5 6 7 8 9 10

This book is dedicated to the memory of the late Reverend Doctor Malachi Martin: friend, confidante, spiritual director, and a faithful servant of Jesus Christ.

TABLE OF CONTENTS

PREFACE

Malachi **Martin.** His name is synonymous in Roman Catholic circles with either steadfast defense of the traditional Church of Rome or occasionally lurid controversy. This book is my effort to unravel the persistent intrigue and bring badly needed truth to the controversies surrounding the late Reverend Doctor Malachi (pronounced Mal-ah-*key*) Martin (hereafter referred to as Malachi) and, in the process, dispel the misconceptions, slander, and outright lies that have sullied his legacy. The original subtitle for this book was *A Prophetic Priest and the Approaching Scream of the Ancient Beast.* That statement referred to Malachi's thesis that Lucifer's insidious takeover of Western Christian culture had its seeds in the sixteenth-century Protestant revolt, the eighteenth-century French Revolution, and the fallen angel's subsequent multi-front assault on the worldwide Roman Catholic Church. As the last man alive who knew Malachi more than just a close friend but also a surrogate grandfather and spiritual director, I've endeavored to bring together the most accurate portrait possible of this oft-maligned twentieth-century giant of Roman Catholicism through the lens of my personal interactions with him.

This is not meant to be an authoritative biography but a personal memoir about a devout priest of Jesus Christ that I knew, respected, and loved like a member of my own family. Additionally, I can now reveal his status as an *in pectore* (secret) bishop and subsequent *in pectore* cardinal, how and why he was trained in "espionage" tradecraft by British intelligence, his travels to minister to the persecuted Catholic Church behind the Soviet "Iron Curtain," and his subsequent torture at the hands of communist secret police. I'll also delve into his claims to know the full Third Secret of Fatima, Satanic worship among senior Vatican clerics, as well as clarify the relationship with his landlady, Mrs. Kakia Livanos. The latter issue has been wielded like a cudgel by his enemies as a "scandal" to discredit Malachi, when, in reality, it was a "nothing burger."

The book's arc pulls from the wide-ranging topics arising from our regular meetings ("meetings"...*that* sounds much too formal. I wonder what a good word is for *"hanging out with my best friend...?"*), conversations, and occasional travel together from 1990 until his tragic, untimely death in 1999. From these, I'll pull the reader into various "scenes" from his life as he related them to me and set the record straight, once and for all, on other controversies I can speak to.

Disclaimer: Although I am an unabashed fan of the late Malachi Martin (how could I *not* be...?), I will present facts regarding Malachi *as they are known to me*. One does not know and regularly interact with a man weekly for almost an entire decade without getting an excellent feeling for the full measure of that man and his character. The same is doubly true as I am a former case officer/operations officer for the Central Intelligence Agency's Clandestine Service. The United States government spent considerable taxpayer dollars to ensure I excelled in my chosen profession. A key part of my skill set was to assess and analyze the personalities of people I met during my day-to-day duties. Malachi's charisma was considerable but did not blind me; instead, the reverse was true. I knew I was in the company of an intellectual giant *and* a holy priest.

Lesser men have tried to sully his reputation since his death with various lurid accusations, but their impotent criticisms will fade into the sands of history as surely as Shelley's *Ozymandias*. Malachi Martin's reputation, on the other hand, will doubtless stand the test of time, refined like gold in a furnace. I do not pretend to be objective. I sincerely believe that one day, when a measure of sanity has been returned to the Roman Catholic Church, and she regains her footing as Christ's beacon to the nations after due procedures are followed, the Reverend Doctor Malachi Brendan Martin will be canonized a saint.

I also have an obligation to Malachi. He introduced me to "hard-identity Catholicism," the authentic Roman Catholic faith as it was taught before the Second Vatican Council. This was the Catholicism that countless martyrs have willingly laid down their lives for, beginning with the Christians who went to the *Circus Maximus* in ancient Rome to be fed to lions or coated in tar and set aflame to illuminate the gladiatorial games rather than drop a pinch of incense over a lamp in front of Caesar's statue. He called it "hard" Catholicism because, in a modern world bent on intellectual and moral compromise, the words and teachings of Jesus of Nazareth require living one's life in fidelity to uncomfortable truth that contradicts modern society. It's not socially acceptable to publicly proclaim Jesus's words in John 14:6 as infallible: *"I am the Way, and the Truth, and the Life. No man cometh to the Father, but by me."*

These are *not* words of tolerance and acceptance, saying that all world faiths are on an equal footing (*as no less than the late Pope Francis himself intimated*), and yet the gentle shepherd from Nazareth said them. To remain faithful in 2025 to the teachings of Jesus of Nazareth demands that a person knowingly subject themselves to accusations of racism, misogyny, sexism, homophobia... and more. Nothing will invoke the wrath of modern culture faster than attempting to live and proclaim authentic fidelity to the teachings of Jesus Christ. Yet I can do no less and still call myself Roman Catholic. This is not said out of pride but of a deep awareness of my faults as a sinner and persevering despite these weaknesses.

1

MEETING MALACHI MARTIN, WHEREIN GOD SETS THE STAGE

A word or two is in order as to what led to meeting the man who literally changed my life. From 1965 through the 1970s, the Catholic Church was marked by change, or more accurately, revolutionary upheaval. The reverberations of this upheaval continue to this day. My fleeting memories of those changes can be encapsulated in the following vignette. It was 1966, and I was in the first grade at Saint Genevieve parochial school in Elizabeth, New Jersey. We six-year-olds in the first grade, led by the redoubtable (and loveably stout) Sister Patricia Murphy, dutifully trooped over to the church for Mass commemorating a long-forgotten Holy Day of Obligation. After the consecration of the Blessed Sacrament (which Catholics hold as an article of faith that a validly ordained priest, through the miracle of transubstantiation, effects the change of the bread and wine into the actual Body, Blood, Soul, and Divinity of Jesus), the pastor, Monsignor Heimbuch, accidentally did the unthinkable: *he accidentally dropped the consecrated host!* By the commotion that broke out on the altar, you would have thought World War III had been announced over the school loudspeaker system. All that we first graders knew was that *Monsignor Heimbuch dropped Jesus!*

I contrast this event with a polar opposite but equally important event in the formation, or more accurately, the *de*formation of my Catholic faith a few years later. We were told that St. Genevieve's Church had to be closed because Pope Paul had ordered changes in the Mass. We were told Mass would temporarily be held in the school cafeteria. *That* Mass was an eye-opener because a group of eighth graders with guitars proceeded to sing decidedly secular songs during Mass. I can distinctly remember songs like Three Dog Night's "Joy to the World" and Cat Stevens's popular rendition of "Morning Has Broken" replacing familiar hymns like "Ave Maria" and "Tantum Ergo." (The more mischievously inclined among us boys took great joy in the discomfiture of the teachers and nuns when we asked them why we couldn't sing *all* of Three Dog Night's "Joy to the World," where the third verse bawdily proclaimed:

> *You know I love the ladies*
> *I love to have my fun*
> *I'm a high-life flyer and a rainbow rider*
> *A straight shootin' son-of-a-gun*

It was nothing earth-shattering, but these songs and the folksy guitars, were followed in a few years by the reception of Holy Communion in the hand and the gradual de-emphasis of sin, forgiveness, and the traditional Four Last Things of Roman Catholicism: Death, Judgment, Heaven, and Hell. Instead, the uniquely Catholic concept of "intimacy with the divine" was gone, replaced with what can only be described as a D-Day style assault of banality. Bedrock Catholic devotions like Adoration of the Blessed Sacrament, recitation of the Rosary, novenas, and various devotions to the Sacred Heart of Jesus and the Immaculate Heart of Mary seemingly vanished overnight and were replaced with the teachings of Teilhard de Chardin, Karl Rahner's concept of 'anonymous Christians, and other heterodox theologians. The takeaway I learned from these 180 degree changes was that there were no absolutes in religion, and the Roman Catholic claim of primacy over all other religions as the "One True Faith" was a load of crap.

So, between the ages of ten and seventeen, my active faith became a vestigial appendage, observed more in the breach than the observance. Sure, I went to weekly Mass, but basically only because my parents held a metaphorical gun to their kid's heads each Sunday morning at 8:30 and ordered us to *"get in the car..."* So, where does Malachi Martin enter the picture? And more to the point, why was he friends with *me*?

As the popular television sitcom title goes, I'm literally "the last man standing" who knew and interacted with Malachi daily for almost a decade. I first became acquainted with him, or rather his work as an author in 1978, during my junior year at Union Catholic High School in Scotch Plains, New Jersey, when I was assigned a book report in religion class. I came across a paperback book by Malachi Martin entitled *Hostage to the Devil: The Story of the Possession and Exorcism of Five Living Americans.* A-*Ha!* Here was a book that appealed to a kid raised on lurid fare like DC comics "Tales From the Crypt" and "Vault of Terror!" Forget religion class and holding hands to sing hippie songs; here was some seriously creepy stuff...and it was REAL. Coming a year or two after William Friedkin's *The Exorcist* managed to scare the living pants off the moviegoing public, this book was just what the doctor ordered for a thrill-seeking high school kid. The irony is that I was to learn many years later that the reality and consequences of possession and exorcism are far more serious and deadly than their portrayal in what Malachi came to derisively call movies like *The Exorcist*: Hollywood Frankenstein and Dracula entertainment that concealed the real dangers behind demonic possession and exorcism.

After devouring *Hostage to the Devil* several times over, I knew that if there was one person I could ever meet, it would be Malachi Martin. Not Yankees slugger Reggie Jackson, Clint Eastwood of *Dirty Harry* fame, Bruce Springsteen, or countless other celebrities of the late 1970s, but *Malachi Martin*. His best-seller appealed to me, not for his intense descriptions of the David-versus-Goliath confrontation that an exorcism entailed, but rather the glimpse it provided me into the Roman Catholic faith that far too many clergy of the late seventies were eager to bury. This was the solid, meat-and-potatoes Catholic faith as it existed before the radical changes introduced in the wake of the Second Vatican Council, or "Vatican II" as it came to be known. I found that the most profound portions of the book were the chapters at the end entitled "Human Spirit and Jesus" and "Human Spirit and Lucifer." I can honestly say I learned more about the central aspects of Roman Catholicism from those two chapters of *Hostage to the Devil* than I did in four years of high school "religious" education.

My desire to meet Malachi Martin would be realized in early 1990 while conducting a routine exercise for the CIA in New York City. On a whim, I went inside the old wooden Gothic Revival Church of the original St. Agnes on East 43rd Street near Grand Central Station prior to its destruction in a devastating fire in December 1992 and was immediately struck by its transcendent beauty. I marveled at the beeswax smell of hundreds of flickering devotional candles mixing with the pungent aroma of incense laced with the sweet, citrusy, balsamic aroma of Frankincense and the rich, earthy scent of Myrrh. The high altar was lit in bright contrast to the dim solemnity enveloping the rest of the church. I was in awe, thinking, *This is where God lives...* The Church of St. Agnes starkly contrasted with the newer 'brutalesque' or theater-in-the-round-style Catholic churches I had been used to until that point.

I soon began attending the Traditional Latin Mass (abbreviated as TLM), the form of the Mass celebrated before the Second Vatican Council each Sunday. Some refer to this Mass as the Tridentine Mass due to a mistaken notion that it was "invented" at the Council of Trent, when, in reality, Trent merely codified a form of liturgy already in existence for centuries. After a few months of regularly attending Sunday Mass at St. Agnes (including one Sunday in 1990, when I left Mass only to find a thug stealing the stereo from my Mazda RX-7 parked outside the church on East 43rd Street) I quickly became quite friendly with the priests assigned to the parish, including one Fr. John Perricone. and the late pastor, Monsignor Eugene Clark.

Father Perricone and I began to occasionally meet for dinner during the week at Empire Szechuan, a popular but excellent, inexpensive Chinese restaurant chain scattered throughout Manhattan. During one of these casual dinners, Fr. Perricone asked what I was reading, and I told him I was halfway through *The Keys of This Blood* by Malachi Martin, a dense geopolitical tome about the centuries-long penetration of the Catholic Church by Communists and Freemasons. Fr. Perricone brightened and said, "Robert, I know Malachi quite well. Would you like to have dinner with him some evening?"

I don't think I could have reacted with more excitement had I been handed a winning lottery ticket. "Would I!?! Of course!"

Fr. Perricone invited me to a dinner event with Malachi at the elegant Isle of Capri restaurant on Third Avenue a few weeks later. Malachi, who cut a dapper, albeit diminutive, white-haired figure in slacks, a sports jacket, and a white turtleneck sweater, arrived without ceremony. I deliberately sat at Malachi's immediate right at the rectangular dinner table, to the obvious jealousy of some seminarians also present for dinner. After referring to Malachi as "Fr.

Martin" several times, I'll never forget when he grabbed my forearm in mock consternation and insisted I call him "Malachi" because I was making him feel like an old man (he was almost seventy at the time).

Afterward, Fr. John gave me Malachi's address so I could mail him a thank-you note and a reciprocal invitation to be my guest for dinner. About a week later, when I arrived home from work, the red light on my answering machine was blinking, and it was Malachi saying he'd be delighted to be my dinner guest. Well, *that* made my week!

Thus began a wonderful friendship featuring countless conversations about many aspects of Malachi's life, travels, and exploits. I also became his *de facto* driver and "Man Friday" whenever he needed to travel by car (which was frequently because he detested the filth and crime of the New York subway system).

From these countless meetings, I've endeavored to craft a modest biographical memoir. The timing is perfect, considering pop culture's enduring fascination with films about the more lurid side of demonic possession and exorcism (*Nefarious, The Exorcist, Deliver Us From Evil, The Pope's Exorcist, The Seventh Day...*), films about Malachi (*Hostage to the Devil, Incident at Fort Bragg*—Lionsgate Films-pre-production), podcasts (*Hostage to the Devil* movie podcasts) and a documentary in production by scholars at Cambridge University in the UK (featuring Malachi's perspectives on the leftist influence of modern heterodox Jesuits), and numerous online interviews with and about Malachi. This non-fiction book will be a natural companion to those seeking to know the truth about one of the most iconic priests ever, the Indiana Jones of the twentieth-century Roman Catholic Church.

Referring to Malachi Martin as the "Indiana Jones of the twentieth-century Roman Catholic Church" is not far off the mark.

Few figures of the twentieth century embody the swashbuckling, globe-trotting spirit of adventure, intellect, and danger quite like the fictional archaeologist Indiana Jones. Yet, examining the life and exploits of Rev. Dr. Malachi Martin, a scholar, archeologist, swordsman, exorcist, spy, polyglot, and Vatican insider, it becomes clear that his life in sum, bore more than a passing resemblance to being a real-world counterpart to Spielberg's legendary character.

In contrast to Indiana Jones, Spielberg's eponymous creation, Malachi Martin was first and foremost a priest and a scholar. While still a young Jesuit, before his 1954 ordination, as a Middle Eastern archaeologist and paleographer (an expert in ancient handwriting), he spent countless hours on his back deciphering proto-Hebrew writings from the time of Abraham deep inside mysterious Sinai Peninsula caves. Malachi later worked extensively on the Dead Sea Scrolls, contributing to one of the most significant biblical and historical discoveries of the twentieth century. His expertise in ancient languages and religious texts mirrored Indiana Jones's fictional background as an academic deeply intrigued by the arcane secrets of ancient civilizations.

And again, in the vein of Indiana Jones, Malachi hated being confined to the dusty libraries of clerical academia; his scholarship had an active, dangerous edge, much like Indy's. His research took him into politically and theologically volatile areas, where his vast knowledge of history and theology often intersected with real-world intrigue. His rapier wit was only matched by his expertise with a real rapier. Whereas Indiana Jones squared off against cunning Nazis in a battle for sacred artifacts, Malachi Martin confronted ruthless communist secret police in a real-life struggle against Marxist oppression. During the Cold War, Martin worked as a covert operative for the Vatican behind the Iron Curtain, evading, sometimes unsuccessfully, communist secret police, smuggling intelligence to the Vatican while offering succor to persecuted Catholics. The stakes in these missions were no less grave than in Spielberg's high-octane thrillers—capture would mean imprisonment, torture, or death.

His role as a Vatican insider and advisor to three popes (John XXIII, Paul VI, and John Paul II) placed him at the heart of ecclesiastical politics, where secrets, power struggles, and theological battles raged. Much like Indiana Jones was called upon to protect sacred relics, Martin worked to defend his sacred, beloved Catholic faith against ideological enemies within and without the Church, always being faithful to the Latin motto of the Jesuit order (the Society of Jesus): *"Ad Majorem Dei Gloriam"* (AMDG), which translates to "For the Greater Glory of God."

In another striking parallel to Indiana Jones, who wielded a bullwhip with legendary ferocity, Malachi was a skilled fencer, a trait that speaks to his discipline, agility, and ability to navigate dangerous situations with intellectual and physical prowess. But his duels were not confined to sabers, rapiers, or geopolitical maneuvering. As a Roman Catholic exorcist, Martin directly confronted the Prince of Darkness and his minions, performing exorcisms that laid bare the terrifying reality of demonic possession. This adds another layer to his Indiana Jones comparison; Jones's adventures often plunged into the supernatural realm, from the Ark of the Covenant to the search for the Holy Grail and the power of ancient relics. Malachi Martin's experiences in spiritual warfare demonstrate that he, too, faced darkness beyond the material world.

Both Indiana Jones and Malachi Martin also possessed an extraordinary command of languages. Jones's linguistic abilities allowed him to decipher ancient scripts, spar with foreign agents, and uncover hidden knowledge. Similarly, Malachi, a master polyglot, used his linguistic skills to conduct deep historical research, advise the Vatican on international matters, and communicate across cultures as a scholar, exorcist, and diplomat.

While Indiana Jones remains a fictional character, Malachi Martin lived a life that, in many ways, rivaled and even exceeded the exploits of Spielberg's cinematic hero. He was a fearless scholar who ventured into the field, a Vatican operative engaged in covert missions, a master of fencing and theology, and a man who stared down the forces of darkness—both ideological and supernatural. If Indiana Jones represents the ideal of a swashbuckling scholar who braved danger for truth and knowledge, then Malachi Martin was not just a worthy comparison; he was quite likely the real thing. For those acquainted with the classic heroism of the Jesuits of old, this shouldn't come as a surprise.

My memory is filled, for the moment, with so many stories of my time with Malachi that it would be a gross injustice to permit this opportunity to slip away. Through the interviews and films mentioned above, there is already an ample body of work on Malachi as an exorcist, and this book will only touch on that subject when it's pertinent. This is not to downplay the reality and dangers of the fascinating, controversial ministry of expelling demons. Instead, I will address the other controversies that dogged Malachi, especially given his outspoken defense of traditional Roman Catholic dogmatic, social, and moral teaching, as well as his prescient condemnation of the madness enveloping Western culture, including the Catholic Church helmed by Pope Leo VIX, known as the "Woke Agenda." As Malachi made clear, the Roman Catholic Church, once a sure bastion against the whims of secular culture, was not immune from these societal toxins. I will make assertions about Malachi as they are facts known to me but that others may find extraordinary or far-fetched by turn.

2

BACKGROUND OF
MALACHI MARTIN

The baby who would one day grow up to become Reverend Doctor Malachi Brendan Martin was born on July 23, 1921, before the founding of the Irish Free State, in the idyllic southeastern seaside town of Ballylongford, County Kerry. Malachi often spoke wistfully of his early childhood with his large family in Ballylongford, likening it to the bucolic village of Innisfree in John Ford's Academy Award–winning 1952 John Wayne classic *The Quiet Man*. He made Ballylongford sound like a miniature paradise to me, with its pastoral scenery, the aroma of fresh-baked scones dripping with salted butter, and strong Irish tea wafting through the narrow village streets. The "wee town," as he called it, sits to this day a stone's throw from the Shannon Estuary and the famed ruins of Carrigafoyle Castle, built in the 1490s by Cornelius O'Connor-Kerry.

Malachi was born prematurely, and his mother, Katherine, experienced a difficult pregnancy with him despite his father Conor being a gynecologist (and an *Englishman* at that). He had Malachi baptized while still in his mother's womb. Therefore, Malachi Martin had the signal grace of entering the world free from Original Sin as an already baptized Roman Catholic *and* a parishioner of Saint Michael's Church in Ballylongford.

Born the eighth of nine children, Malachi had four sisters and four brothers: Netta, Kathleen, Joan, Maura, Francis Xavier, Liam, Conor, and Jimmy. His youngest brother, Jimmy, died while he was still a child; Malachi never told me the cause of his youngest brother Jimmy's death. The four surviving brothers all went on to join the Catholic priesthood, receiving a variety of clerical accolades in the process. Malachi regaled me with stories of how, as a child, he and his brothers would escape their stern father's watchful eye and steal off to the ruins of Carrigafoyle Castle, pretending to be brave Irish and Spanish troops defending the castle against the ruthless English Protestant armies of Queen Elizabeth I and Oliver Cromwell.

When Malachi was a young boy, his father moved the family to Dublin in 1931, where Dr. Conor Martin expanded his medical practice well beyond what the remote Ballylongford permitted. Around ten years old, before discerning a religious vocation, Malachi and his family became parishioners of Saint Agatha's Church in Dublin. Malachi then joined the Society of Jesus, a.k.a. the Jesuits, in 1940 at eighteen and attended Dublin's Belvedere College.

Malachi's academic journey was a testament to his intellectual prowess and insatiable thirst for knowledge. He earned his bachelor's degrees in Semitic Languages and Oriental History and then embarked on a journey to Belgium, where he attended the prestigious University of Louvain. There, he delved deeper into philosophy, theology, ancient Semitic languages, archeology, paleography, and Oriental history. His quest led him to Hebrew University in Jerusalem and Oxford University in the UK, where he specialized in "inter-testamentary studies" and deepened his understanding of Jesus through ancient Hebrew and Arabic writings. His academic pursuits also extended to anthropology, psychology, and physics.

Malachi's academic prowess and talent in paleography (where he specialized in Semitic written languages around the time of the Hebrew patriarch Abraham) were put to use in his role as one of the earliest researchers to perform analytic translation work on the renowned Dead Sea Scrolls. In 1958, he published his first work, a two-volume set entitled *The Scribal Character of the Dead Sea Scrolls*. His academic achievements, which spanned multiple disciplines and culminated in groundbreaking research, inspired admiration and respect from his academic peers.[1]

Despite the demanding pace of his academic and research work, which would have overwhelmed lesser men, Malachi remained unwavering in his commitment to his faith. He completed his studies for the priesthood and was ordained to the priesthood on August 15, 1954 (the Feast of the Assumption) by Cardinal Leo Joseph Suenens, then Archbishop of Mechelen-Brussels. His ordination took place at the Cathedral of St. Rombold in Mechelen, Belgium. In the face of his other obligations, this remarkable feat is a testament to Malachi's unwavering determination and the depth of his spiritual determination to follow in the footsteps of his beloved Lord Jesus. His commitment to his faith, even during his academic pursuits, is a source of reverence and admiration to those interested in religious history and academia.

Before the onset of the Second Vatican Council, Malachi became an aide to the German Jesuit Cardinal Augustin Bea. Malachi told me although Cardinal Bea was considered a "liberal" at the Second Vatican Council, compared to theologians and clergy of the 1990s, Bea would today be on the same conservative ideological wavelength as Cardinal Ratzinger, prefect of the former Congregation of the Doctrine of the Faith (CDF) and later Pope Benedict XVI.

---

1.   Martin, Malachi (1958), *The Scribal Character of the Dead Sea Scrolls*, Bibliothèque du Muséon, Louvain: Publications Universitaires, 2 volumes.

Malachi always got a chuckle because Cardinal Ratzinger was alternately portrayed by liberal media, secular and religious, as the "Panzer Cardinal" or the "Pope's Rottweiler." Malachi thought it ironic because during his CDF tenure, Cardinal Ratzinger only levied canonical sanctions against a few individuals, and these tended to be the most egregious offenders against Catholic doctrine, such as the late Father Edward Schillebeeckx, the outspoken heterodox priest at the Dutch University of Nijmegen and the late Father Tissa Balasuriya. While Schillebeeckx was only disciplined and warned about his writings, Father Balasuriya persisted in defiance of Catholic dogma until he formally incurred the penalty of excommunication in 1997. (Balasuriya was later reconciled with the Church, and his excommunication was lifted.)

Due to his expertise in ancient Semitic languages, especially Hebrew and Aramaic, Malachi was seen as an indispensable interlocutor with Jewish religious leaders at Cardinal Bea's request during the Second Vatican Council. This ultimately gave rise to unfounded rumors that Malachi Martin was a secret agent for the Israeli *Mossad* intelligence service.

As a Jesuit priest, the liberalizing trends that came to the fore during Vatican II ultimately proved to be the proverbial "last straw" for Malachi and his association with his beloved Jesuits. He observed and later documented in his tell-all book *The Jesuits: The Society of Jesus and the Betrayal of the Roman Catholic Church* the steady leftward drift of the Society of Jesus past liberalism into the waiting secular embrace of Gramscian Marxism.

Antonio Gramsci (b. 1891 d. 1937) was a Sardinian Marxist political philosopher, who founded the Italian Communist Party and whose political thought regarding how the Communist revolution and the "workers' paradise" could be effectively implemented put him at odds with Soviet Russian Communists such as Joseph

Stalin. He created the dual paradigms of Communist revolution. The first was a *War of Maneuver*: a direct, violent revolution, like the 1917 Bolshevik Revolution in Russia. The second, and Gramsci's preferred alternative, was a *War of Position*: a methodical, ideological, and cultural struggle to shift overall public consciousness before a political revolution could take place.

Gramsci argued that in advanced capitalist societies, revolutions require a long-term ideological battle, not just armed insurrection. He viewed the *transcendent* elements of Roman Catholicism as an obstacle to revolutionary consciousness because they directed people's hopes away from a purely this-world material reality. Gramsci strongly repudiated the Church's fundamental dogma that man was created to serve a transcendent God and to abide with Him in eternity after death. However, he respected the Church's ability to organize, educate, and mobilize people, a strength he thought Marxists should study and emulate. Instead of fighting religion outright, he believed in constructing a new secular worldview in Roman Catholicism that could inspire and mobilize people toward socialism. In Gramsci's view, Jesus was not the Son of God but the archetype of the workers' proletariat, killed not to atone for sin but to demonstrate to the working classes the evils of capitalism. The Virgin Mary was no longer the Mother of God; she became the "Mother of the Proletariate." Taken to its logical conclusion, it was Catholicism emptied of transcendence, and to his dismay, Malachi saw his fellow Jesuits, either wittingly or unwittingly, embrace Gramscian ideals in a flawed application of social justice principles in the years leading up to the Second Vatican Council.

His exposé of the leftist changes within the Jesuit Order earned him considerable *opprobrium* from the liberal media *and* within the Jesuit order itself. In 1964, Malachi petitioned Pope Paul VI to be released from the Jesuits as he could no longer reconcile his orthodox Roman Catholic beliefs with the gale force winds of Gramscian Marxist change blowing through the Jesuit Order. Paul VI granted Malachi's request in 1965 via a papal document called a *rescript*, which Malachi compared to an Executive Order by the president of the United States. In Malachi's case, his *rescript* released him from his vow of obedience so he could leave the Jesuits, and from his vow of poverty so Malachi could earn a living as a writer. As a now secular priest, he was still bound by his vow of chastity, although his detractors, not least of whom were Jesuits, continued to levy lurid allegations of sexual impropriety against Malachi Martin right up until his death.

Although now a secular priest, leaving Rome, Malachi began a trek in late 1964 that landed him first in Paris and then with his family in Ireland, where his persecutors among the Jesuits pursued him. Anticipating that Malachi would seek solace with his family, they tried to convince his relatives, especially his sister Netta, that Malachi had left Rome and the Jesuits because he was suffering from severe mental illness and had a nervous breakdown. Malachi then left Ireland to go to New York City. I recall a particularly rough patch in my life after my service with the U.S. government had ended, and I was finding it very hard to find a job, when Malachi gave me a charitable dose of what today would be called "tough love." When I lamented that I couldn't find a suitable "executive job" befitting my ego, Malachi came right out and told me that when he first arrived in New York City, he was practically penniless and had to work two jobs simultaneously. His first job in Manhattan was washing dishes and cleaning out grease traps in a Greenwich Village donut shop for $1.25 an hour, and to supplement this meager income, he drove a taxicab by night.

Malachi left these jobs behind when he received his first Guggenheim Fellowship in 1967, which enabled him to publish his first American-authored book, *The Encounter: Religions in Crisis*. The key theme of this book was that modern faiths, but above all Roman Catholicism, needed to be wary in their efforts to modernize Catholic doctrine in their efforts to remain relevant in the face of advancing secularism. He feared this would lead to internal division and a loss of spiritual authenticity. This first foray into the American literary landscape earned Malachi the first of many accolades for his books, in this case, the Choice Book Award of the American Library Association. He received another Guggenheim Fellowship in 1970 and set about building a career as a full-time author. A quick perusal of Google will bring up his plethora of works, from *The Encounter* to his penultimate and most controversial book, the "factional" novel *Windswept House*. Like his other novels, Malachi used the term faction, a portmanteau combination of "fact" and "fiction," wherein a fictional story speaks of true events, to describe several of his novels in addition to *Windswept House*, including *The Final Conclave* and *Vatican*. This literary genre originated in the 1930s and was also used by literary luminaries such as Taylor Caldwell, Norman Mailer, and Jeffrey Archer.

Malachi's final book, most definitely *not* a faction, was published in 2020. It is entitled *A Priest and His Dog: The Tale of Tati*. This short book tells the heart-wrenching story of how Malachi firmly believed the Lord Jesus used the most humble of creatures, a small cairn terrier puppy named Tati, to bring the warmth of humanity more fully into Malachi's heart, a humanity Malachi himself believed his rigorous Jesuit training had purged him of years earlier. This was evidenced by Malachi's own admission that he didn't shed a tear at the wake or funeral of his beloved mother, Katherine. Tati's influence on Malachi was such that she merits her own chapter later in this book. Tati aside, Malachi's budding literary fame in the early 1970s and his towering intellect initially brought him steady work as an editor at the Manhattan offices of the prestigious *Encyclopedia Brittanica* and later as the religion editor for William F. Buckley's *National Review* magazine.

Buckley immediately and intuitively saw the value a brilliant intellect like Malachi's could bring to *National Review* and, later, Buckley's celebrated public television series *Firing Line*. His appearances on *Firing Line* are still available on YouTube, made possible by the generosity of the Hoover Institute at Stanford University.

Malachi was a polymath *and* a polyglot, fluent in numerous languages. These languages were English, Latin, Italian, Classical and Koine Greek, Hebrew, Aramaic, Arabic, French, German, and Spanish. Classical Greek was the language spoken by Plato and Aristotle, while Koine Greek was the language spoken in the centuries immediately before and after the time Jesus walked the earth. Koine Greek was the common tongue of the ancient Middle East, as it served as a "bridge language" to facilitate trade, diplomacy, governance, or other interactions in multilingual regions such as ancient Judea.

It's fitting that Malachi's favorite physical sport was fencing, for his skill with an actual rapier was only matched by his rapier-sharp wit. There's an anecdotal story told of Malachi that while he was an aide to Cardinal Bea before leaving Rome in 1965, he learned to verbally wield Roman power as effectively as a sword. He said there were times when he, ostensibly a mere priest and aide to Cardinal Bea, could make powerful cardinals in the Roman Curia sweat...*and he enjoyed it*. This speaks to a politically ruthless side of Malachi that I was never privy to, and I'm glad for it. The Malachi Martin I met in 1990 was not an arrogant prig but a genial, grandfatherly man and kindly priest, overflowing with a sincere love of his cherished Roman Catholic Church and charity towards his fellow man. He was marked by his unwavering determination to speak out with the clarion call of the lone watchman on the wall of the dangers threatening late twentieth-century Roman Catholicism. He wore his love for the Lord Jesus and His mother, the Blessed Virgin Mary, especially under her title of Our Lady of Fatima, proudly on his sleeve.

For all his acclaim as a celebrity author and media commentator, Malachi retained an authentic "everyman's touch," where no one was too trivial for him to take a sincere interest in. I often accompanied him on lunchtime strolls around his Upper East Side neighborhood while he ran sundry errands to his stationer or the dry cleaner. It became the norm when New Yorkers from all walks of life strolled by, from building janitors and doormen to NYPD officers to cabbies shouting in their Brooklyn accent, "Hey, Faddah Martin...!" to greet him. Depending on who recognized him, it was always either "Doctor Martin" or "Father Martin." Malachi must have had a photographic memory because he would bring up minute details of their lives drawn from these conversations, whether it was the nurse working at Lenox Hill Hospital with an alcoholic husband, the cop living paycheck to paycheck with an autistic son, or the taxi driver struggling to obtain a mortgage to buy his family a way out of a run-down Lower East Side tenement. They always left the briefest encounter with Malachi heartened and consoled, and *always* with a promise by Malachi to pray for them. His book of Mass intentions overflowed with the names of these sundry New Yorkers. Although no stranger to the *glitterati* of the New York literary scene, other than the Lord Jesus and His Mother, love of everyday people took pride of place in Malachi Martin's heart. One promise I know he always kept was that if Malachi said he would pray for you, he *did*.

A bit of explanation is in order here. Every Catholic priest is called to be an *alter Christus*, Latin for "another Christ." At a valid Roman Mass, when the priest says the words of Consecration over the bread and wine, according to the beliefs of the Roman Catholic Church, the priest is acting *in persona Christi* or "in the person of Christ." Through the power and authority of Jesus bestowed on him through ordination by the Church, the priest changes the bread and wine into the Body, Blood, Soul, and Divinity of Jesus. Malachi told me that when a Catholic priest is ordained, there is an indelible change imprinted on their soul by Christ. I recall from reading the biblical accounts how crowds would follow Jesus from town to town or how throngs would be waiting on the shore of the Sea of Galilee, drawn by Christ's divine charisma. I believe Malachi, upon his ordination, pronounced his own *fiat voluntas tua* or "thy will be done" to his Savior on the cross. In return, in addition to conferring priestly power and authority, I believe Jesus gratuitously also gave Malachi a droplet of His divine charisma. I can find no other reason why people were so drawn to him. As Malachi's tiny apostolate spread from his little cubby to souls worldwide through his books, radio interviews, or media appearances, people inexplicably knew this was a *"man of God"* and were drawn to him accordingly.

In his later years, the 1980s and 1990s, Malachi restricted himself to the three parts of his work he considered most important: his writing, performing or assisting at exorcisms, and media appearances, whether his formal, structured interviews with Bernard Janzen of the Canadian Catholic media firm Triumph Communications or his appearances on Sean Hannity's 770WABC syndicated drive-time radio show or the late Art Bell's famed *Coast to Coast AM* late night radio show. At the time, Hannity had a drive-time audience of up to two million listeners, and Art Bell's audience ranged from fifteen to sixteen million people via five hundred AM radio stations across the United States and Canada. Malachi's detractors often try to use his appearances on *Coast to Coast AM* as fodder for attacks against Malachi, given the occasionally downright ludicrous guests on the show, but Malachi believed in reaching as many souls as possible and took every opportunity to do so. Sean Hannity and Art Bell were on record that Malachi Martin was one of their most popular guests and kept their switchboards jammed when he was their guest.

Many people continued to believe the slander that Malachi had been laicized and was, therefore, no longer a Catholic priest. I remember back in the 1990s, Father Mitch Pacwa frequently hung up on callers to his EWTN show when people asked about Malachi's status. Pacwa would alternately have a look of disgust or a smirk of supercilious contempt on his face.

In 2004, Father Tom Widner, SJ, secretary for communications of the U.S. Jesuit Conference, refuted the slander against Malachi's status as a still-licit Catholic priest until Malachi's passing. In order to set the record straight, Widner questioned the late Father Vincent O'Keefe, SJ, former vicar general of the Society of Jesus and a past president of Fordham University, about Malachi's status as a priest. O'Keefe affirmed that Malachi Martin was, in fact, granted a dispensation from all his vows in the Jesuit order except for chastity. Father O'Keefe was the vicar general of the Society in 1965, at the time of Father Malachi Martin's departure from Rome. It is unknown why Father O'Keefe set the record straight on Malachi Martin; perhaps in his twilight years, his conscience was bothering him.

I do not doubt Malachi's status as a priest, as I served as his impromptu altar server for many Masses conducted in private homes for the beleaguered faithful. Another fact that testifies to Malachi's good standing in the Vatican of Pope John Paul II is that in June 1995, Malachi arranged, with a mere phone call to Rome, for me to attend a semi-private audience with the pope and about twenty other people just before Pope John Paul II's Wednesday general audience in the Nervi Hall. To this day, I have a picture taken by a

Vatican photographer of my much younger self handing Pope John Paul II a pen-and-ink rendition of Our Lady of Fatima. His Holiness and I were mere inches apart, all because of a single phone call placed by Malachi to Rome.

3

THE IRISH SCOUT MEETS
DER FUHRER AND IL DUCE

As a teenage member of the CBSI (Catholic Boy Scouts of Ireland, in Gaelic, the *Gasóga Catoilici na hÉireann*), Malachi's scout troop accepted an invitation to meet the rising dictators of Germany and Italy, Adolf Hitler and Benito Mussolini, during a European tour circa early 1934. Although Malachi had yet to enter his Jesuit formation, his keen spiritual discernment and Guardian Angel gave him an interior warning of the preternatural darkness at work in the souls of these men.

Malachi related how his CBSI scout troop took a trip to continental Europe, where the highlights of the trip were official audiences with Adolf Hitler, the chancellor of Nazi Germany, and Benito Mussolini, the fascist prime minister of Italy. At this time, Adolf Hitler was still consolidating his power over Germany, transforming it from the failed Weimar Republic into the fearsome belligerent that would go on to conquer most of continental Europe less than a decade later. For context, this trip took place barely twelve years after Ireland achieved its independence from the United Kingdom in 1922. There was no love lost between the UK and Germany (or fascist Italy) in the years following World War I. This could also accurately describe the situation before and after Ireland won independence from the United Kingdom in the Anglo-Irish Treaty of 1921. This treaty was preceded by several years of brutal guerilla warfare between the Irish Republican Army and British forces immediately after the end of World War I. Deep animosity remained towards Britain throughout Irish society due to atrocities committed by both the British Army and their companion police force, the RIC (Royal Irish Constabulary). One of the most infamous of these incidents was the 1920 "Bloody Sunday" massacre where fourteen civilians were killed and an estimated sixty to one hundred injured when British forces opened fire on the crowd at a soccer match in Dublin between teams from Dublin and Tipperary. The legacy of this infamous event has lived on in popular culture as one of the two "Bloody Sunday" events (the other being the 1972 "Bloody Sunday" massacre by the British Army in Ulster). The Irish mega rock band U2 referenced the 1920 Bloody Sunday as one of the inspirations for the song that made them international superstars in 1983, "Sunday, Bloody Sunday."

Following the old maxim, *"the enemy of my enemy is my friend,"* the Irish CBSI scouts set off for Germany. After arriving in Berlin, they were put up in a youth hostel near the Wilhelmstraße district. The Wilhelmstraße was interchangeable for the seat of the German government. In earlier times, it was home to the minister for the Royal Household and the Prussian State Ministry; however, under the rule of the Nazi Party, it also held the chancellery, the Ministry of Finance, the Ministries of Food and Transport, and the Foreign Office. Within a few years, the district would also house the office complex for the Reich Ministry of Aviation and official seat of its minister, Hermann Göring.

Malachi told me how, the day after arriving in Berlin, the Irish scouts were shepherded into a large ornate room within an imposing building in the Wilhelmstraße district. He related how the young

Irish CBSI scouts were ushered into the presence of *"Der Führer,"* and Hitler greeted each Irish scout in turn all standing in line. He related, contrary to what someone might think upon meeting a man as profoundly evil as Adolph Hitler, that *"Der Führer"* was quite cordial and put them all at ease. It was only the young Malachi Martin who heard what he described to me as "spiritual alarm bells going off in my head..." He later attributed this spiritual consternation to his own Guardian Angel warning the young scout of Hitler's diabolical nature. In his later years, after his ordination as a priest, Malachi became convinced this deep sense of spiritual unease and discomfort he experienced was a warning from his Guardian Angel that he was in the presence of deeply profound evil. During one of our lunches, Malachi told me he believed Adolph Hitler to be what exorcists call "perfectly possessed." Among exorcists, perfect possession is said to occur when a person freely gives control of their very self over to Lucifer with full consent of their will. In this context, a perfectly possessed person could attend Mass, receive the Holy Eucharist, and dip their hands into a holy water font without exhibiting a single outward sign of distress.

Despite his ghastly later legacy (Malachi told me that he believed Hitler to be one of the forerunners of the Antichrist mentioned in the Bible), Hitler evinced none of the preternatural signs often associated with demonic possession; he appeared perfectly at ease with the young scouts and their chaperones. He told me that the scout troop's audience with Hitler lasted only about fifteen minutes, and the impression left on the young Malachi was that immensely powerful evil could be cloaked in a reassuring sense of outward normalcy. Young Malachi's spiritual senses, although still inchoate and not yet really developed, still had enough spiritual acumen to recognize the presence of the Devil embedded in one of his servants.

After meeting Hitler, Malachi's CBSI scouts traveled by train to Rome for their meeting with the fascist dictator of Italy, Benito Mussolini. After spending two nights cooling their heels in a Roman youth hostel, Malachi told me an early-morning summons had come by an official courier of the fascist government on their third day in Rome; they would meet *Il Duce* that day at noon in a reception hall at the Palazzo Venezia. Malachi told me how, after meeting the banality of evil in Adolf Hitler, it was obvious that Mussolini had a healthy ego and a very high opinion of himself, almost like a showman or entertainer. Instead of standing in a receiving line as they had done in Berlin, Italian fascist protocol dictated that each scout would have to walk down an approximately sixty-five-foot-long reception hall where Mussolini sat at the end of the cavernous room. Mussolini sat atop a throne-like chair with his jaw jutting out, flanked by armed guards in ornate uniforms where the Irish scouts walked up to be introduced to him individually.

Malachi told me that Benito Mussolini would carefully observe someone as they walked up to be introduced. He said this is how Mussolini took the measure of a man and judged his character. If the person walked up with a straight back, his head held up confidently, and maintained eye contact with the fascist dictator, then Mussolini would accord that person a modicum of respect. The opposite was also true. If your gaze was downcast and your overall demeanor lacked confidence, *Il Duce* would already be looking over your shoulder to see who the next person to approach him would be. Unlike Hitler, who Malachi said radiated evil, Mussolini just gave off the impression that "he was your mean uncle who beat his wife," as Malachi put it. One comment Malachi remembered from a fellow Irish scout about both meetings was "that Hitler feller gives ya a right good case of the willies, but Mussolini just has a mug beggin' fer a good punch...."

4

INSIDE THE DEVIL'S DUNGEON

Special Prisoner 23486 softly moaned as pain flooded his body while crouched in the cramped underground detention cell Number 45 of Lviv's infamous Prison on Lontskoho Street this February 1, 1957. Formerly known as Lviv NKVD Prison No.1, now run by the Ukrainian Soviet KGB secret police, many nameless souls entered its walls, never to be seen or heard from again. But Special Prisoner 23486 was indeed *special*. He had recently arrived by train, escorted by three KGB counterintelligence agents who had traveled to Prague, Czechoslovakia, where he was handed over to the Soviets by the Czechoslovakian Communist State Security Service (StB) agents. The frustration on the faces of the Czech StB agents clearly showed as they handed their shackled charge over to the quietly waiting KGB agents.

Over the past six weeks, the Czech StB agents tried everything in their toolkit of torture and intimidation to extract a confession from the mute Special Prisoner 23486 but were frustrated at every turn. Czechoslovakia's post–World War II agents considered themselves a new breed of secret police, dedicated communists in the vanguard of Communism who learned their malign craft from interrogation experts at KGB headquarters on Lubyanka Square in Moscow. Grim experts in torture and interrogation, including coarser methods of beatings, sleep deprivation, and the use of psychoactive drugs, they had been singularly unable to break the will of this prisoner. The StB had been alerted to his presence in Prague several weeks earlier when a turncoat priest from the outlawed Czech underground Catholic Church had called them in a fit of resentment and bitterness. The turncoat informed them, "he had just been the subject of an unannounced and intimidating visit by a mysterious stranger from Rome, who claimed to be a bishop sent by none other than Pope Pius XII himself. He was mumbling some nonsense that he was going to excommunicate me."

In his fit of rage, the turncoat was right, of course. The slight figure cut by the young Jesuit, now in KGB custody and headed for an uncertain fate at best, was consecrated five months earlier as a secret bishop of the Roman Catholic Church by Bishop Domenico Tardini, the Vatican Pro-Secretary of State for Extraordinary Ecclesiastical Affairs, with the express approval of Pope Pius XII. After the brief ceremony in Rome's Church of the Twelve Holy Apostles, or *Santi Apostoli* as the Italian locals called it, Bishop Tardini, and two weeks later, Pope Pius XII himself, gave the newly consecrated *episcopus in pectore*, or secret bishop, a direct, almost perfunctory briefing of the situation that awaited the new Bishop Malachi Martin, SJ.

Tardini came right to the point.

"Your Excellency," he began in Italian. "You know well the great difficulties we have had in sustaining the Church in Eastern Europe after the Soviets and their Red Army took control after the war. We have many brave men and women who risk their lives each day to keep the light of Our Lord Jesus's Church burning not only in the few churches we are permitted but also in the hearts of the faithful. Our own Augustin Bea himself, one of your fellow Jesuits, has himself run the gauntlet of communist authorities taking the pulse of the underground Church in the nations enslaved by Moscow. Now, with the collapse of our efforts in Hungary after the Soviets' brutal suppression of the workers' revolt, the sustenance of the remaining Church at large in the European lands held captive by the Soviets becomes a matter of paramount importance. His Holiness is determined to thwart the efforts of that coarse little Ukrainian Khrushchev to stamp out the flame of faith.

"You are aware of our efforts to build an underground church in these countries, no?" Tardini raised an eyebrow at Bishop Martin. "A singular problem has arisen in Czechoslovakia. We have received information that a priest of the underground Church in Prague, one Father Jan Tomáš Kadlec, has not only taken a wife in violation of his vow of chastity but has also fathered triplets with this woman. Needless to say, this has caused great distress and scandal among his little flock, already suffering privation at the hands of their Soviet overlords. When Father Kadlec's superior, Bishop Hlonoc, reprimanded him and told him that he had to choose between his service to Christ or the woman Father Kadlec married in a civil ceremony, Father Kadlec refused to do either. In fact, Father Kadlec ignored Bishop Hlonoc's admonishment and said if His Excellency attempted to impose a canonical punishment, Kadlec would denounce him to the communist authorities. Bishop Hlonoc hastily left Father Kadlec's apartment and sent us word of his predicament."

Although he intuited the answer, the new Bishop Martin blinked through his glasses riding low on his nose and asked anyway.

"And what is my role in this situation, Your Excellency?"

Tardini got right to the point.

"Given your years of work in refugee resettlement and nurturing the Church in Soviet-occupied Europe after the recent war, His Holiness thinks you are uniquely qualified to resolve this unfortunate situation. You will travel to Prague in suitable disguise as the direct representative of His Holiness and go to this Father Kadlec. If he refuses to see the light of reason, the pope has authorized you to remove his priestly faculties and reduce him to an ordinary layman."

Bishop Martin nodded his assent.

"When do I leave?"

Tardini informed the newly minted bishop that he first had to undergo deeper "familiarization" with how things worked in the underground church behind what Winston Churchill had dubbed the "Iron Curtain" of Soviet-occupied Eastern Europe. Previously, Father Martin's trips to the captive nations had been overt trips on behalf of the Holy See, but now he was stepping into the dangerous world of undercover work on behalf of the fragile underground Church. Tardini looked Malachi in the eye and said, "Do you remember Our Lord's words to His disciples in Matthew 10:15?"

Malachi looked Tardini in the eye with his detached Jesuitical gaze and replied with the Scriptural reference: *"Behold I send you as sheep in the midst of wolves. Be ye therefore wise as serpents and simple as doves. But beware of men. For they will deliver you up...."* Martin knew he would be the sheep and the Soviet KGB secret police the wolves.

Henceforth, Malachi would be on his own, but not without preparation. The day after his consecration as a bishop, Tardini introduced Malachi to a small group of men who would facilitate his covert infiltration into Communist-occupied Europe. He quickly discerned that the men were from two separate organizations: British MI6 SIS (Secret Intelligence Service) officers and U.S. Air Force pararescue specialists, who would teach the young cleric covert parachute insertion techniques into hostile territory. Given the historical animosity between the British and the Irish, Malachi found it more than ironic that he depended on these two burly "Brits" to provide him with training designed to save his life. For five weeks, they relentlessly drilled him in the art of making himself "invisible" to Czech or Soviet secret police. The key was sticking to his "legend," or cover story, under any circumstance. Given their well-deserved reputation in counter-espionage, especially through the infamous Stalin-era SMERSH organization (Smert' Shpionam or "Death to Spies"), and later merged into the MGB, then the KGB, the Soviets would pick up on any discrepancy, no matter how small, as a pretext to arrest him. Malachi had to pay attention to the slightest details, his manner of walking and talking, what hand he used to pick up eating utensils, and so on, to blend in. Malachi had to transform himself into a non-threatening "nobody." His MI6 instructors taught him how to travel under the cover of a rare religious book dealer for the Vatican Museums.

Although Malachi would later tell people that he was posted to Incirlik Air Force Base as a chaplain for U.S. airmen stationed there who manned U.S. listening posts oriented across the Black Sea towards the Soviet Union, his real destination was actually Aviano, Italy. He traveled north from Rome to the joint Italian–U.S. Air Force Aviano Air Base at the foot of the Southern Carnic Alps. There he spent weeks training in the dangerous art of low-altitude parachute jumping. The trick, the Americans told him, was to hit the ground the way a drunken man topples over and *never* try to land on his feet, as that would practically guarantee broken ankles. The only parachutists who landed on their feet were in Hollywood movies.

Finally, the day came when Malachi would put his training to use. As dusk approached on the evening of October 15, Malachi walked with his instructors and flight crew to a waiting Douglas C-47 "Gooney Bird" outfitted with special Pratt and Whitney engines designed to suppress the aircraft's noise. The aircraft had no markings to show its country of origin. His MI6 trainers and U.S. Air Force parachutist instructors exchanged silent glances that said, "Better him than us."

The blacked-out C-47 flew low over the Alps and across neutral Austrian territory at low altitude, north towards Haugschlag, through a small, low-altitude gap in Soviet air defense radar coverage. The C-47 flew over a primitive airstrip near Divišov, Czechoslovakia, about thirty-five miles southeast of Prague, where Bishop Martin bid farewell to his American friends and leaped into the cold night. He was met on the ground by a gruff peasant named Milos, who greeted him with the whispered first part of a prearranged code phrase, "When misty ivy falls..." Malachi responded with, "over sleepy garden walls." Malachi was quickly bundled into a waiting car and driven thirty-five miles to Prague, exchanging no conversation with his escort. An hour later, the sedan pulled up next to a taxi idling with its lights off in a grimy industrial suburb of Prague that still showed scars from Allied bombardment during the war just over a decade earlier. Malachi quickly entered the taxi, and after a similar exchange of coded introductory phrases, the driver introduced himself as Bishop Anton Hlonoc, taxi driver by day and Pope Pius XII's *sub-rosa* Apostolic representative "amidst the Soviet wolves" by night.

"Bishop Tardini briefed you on our dilemma, Your Excellency?" Bishop Hlonoc asked. Malachi realized word of his elevated status as an *in pectore* bishop had already reached the underground Church hierarchy, despite the omnipresent Soviet security apparatus. Malachi nodded.

"Then you know you're walking into the lion's den, Bishop Martin. I've tried to reason with Father Kadlec; however, his position is quite intractable. Despite his properly contracted civil marriage, from the perspective of Holy Mother Church, he is violating his vows of chastity by living in sin with a woman in a state of adultery. Your presence here means the Vatican sees only one course of action: give Father Kadlec a final chance to repent or laicize Father

Kadlec and remove him from the priesthood. I fully expect him to call the police as soon as you depart his flat. He is immature and petulant, aware of his sin but unwilling to repent. As for the rest of my priests, they are already hidden in safe houses, and I shall soon be as well. May the Holy Virgin watch over you, Bishop Martin."

Malachi Martin exited the taxi, which sped off, and walked the ten circuitous blocks to Father Kadlec's apartment house.

Father Kadlec took the unexpected visit from the newly minted Bishop Martin with the same rude incivility he had shown Bishop Hlonoc.

"Rome, eh?" Kadlec spat out. "I already work myself to the bone twelve hours a day in the Zlasava Iron Works, providing for my wife, Marta, and our children. Then I spend half the night listening to people confess nonsense or sprinkling holy water over babies and the dying. Look around you, *Your Excellency*," he spat out. "This isn't the luxury of the Vatican. Those eunuchs in Rome can kiss my ass." After informing the recalcitrant priest he was now a layman, the young Bishop Malachi Martin wasn't halfway down the block outside the Kadlec's apartment building before Czech StB agents waylaid him and bundled him into a waiting car. The now former *Father* Kadlec had made good on his threat.

That was only the beginning of Malachi's ordeal at the hands of the StB. Two straight months of interrogation, beatings, and torture had not broken the will of their Jesuit prisoner. It had left him with numerous broken bones, welts, scars, cardiac damage, and damage to his psyche, but still, he had not betrayed the identities of the underground Catholic churchmen in Communist Czechoslovakia. Finally, the exasperated Czech StB admitted defeat and grudgingly turned the young Bishop Malachi Martin over to their Soviet KGB overlords. After a grueling trip in a special KGB rail car with a hood roughly yanked over his head, the young Jesuit and his KGB captors arrived at an entrance to the Lviv KGB main headquarters and prison on Lontskoho Street.

Months of brutal KGB interrogation followed Malachi's initial meeting with the local KGB commander. His superiors in Rome assumed the worst when he did not leave a prearranged sign at a location in Prague that he had met with Father Kadlec and was returning to Rome.

Although Malachi was reticent to tell me every detail of the cruelty inflicted on him by his KGB captors, he did admit that he was subject to extended sleep deprivation, starvation, exposure to extreme cold (winters in Ukraine are very harsh), beatings on the soles of his feet with rubber truncheons, and being forced to stand upright for days at a time in a closet-sized cell. He also spoke of two other notable cruelties inflicted on him.

The first was being forced to stand in a concrete cell that measured approximately three feet deep, four feet tall, and four feet wide. There was nowhere in the cell to sit, and the floor was tilted at roughly forty-five degrees. The bottom half of the tilted floor was submerged in icy water so that when the standing prisoner fell asleep from sheer exhaustion, he would tumble into the icy water, instantly awakening him with a shock. A KGB guard supervised this process as it was repeated indefinitely to ensure the prisoner didn't succumb and drown in the water punishment cell. The prisoner was then taken before his interrogator, who would affect different demeanors from friendly to threatening to get the prisoner to confess or, at the very least, slip up.

The KGB's second torture method on the young cleric was even more brutal. It consisted of having the prisoner stripped of his uniform, with the possible exception of his thin shirt, and hung by his bound wrists from an iron hook set in the ceiling. In most cases, the tips of his feet barely touched the floor. The prisoner was doused with several large buckets of icy water before his interrogator entered wearing heavy rubber boots, thick insulated gloves, a leather apron, and holding the prison equivalent of an electric cattle prod. Questions were put to the prisoner, and when he remained mute, the KGB interrogator methodically applied the electric prod to various parts of his body, concentrating on his genitalia and anus. Malachi told me the pain was indescribable, that his body would spasm in ways he didn't think the human form could contort into. From what he could tell, Malachi said that a sizable number of these KGB interrogators would get blind drunk at the end of each day, perhaps in a vain attempt to drown their inhumanity in alcohol.

When he recounted these experiences to me during our lunches, I never doubted him. After all, Malachi said he would obtain an audience for me with (now) Pope Saint John Paul II, and he did. Also, as a CIA operations officer, I was fully aware of what the KGB could dole out, especially in search of information. What alternately grieved and infuriated me was that my friend had to endure any of this in the first place. Second, Malachi Martin never broke under either StB or KGB interrogative torture, even when his torturers anally raped him with a cattle prod. I remember asking Malachi how the Vatican could be sure he was never compromised and "turned" by his communist captors. He replied that if he had succumbed to the KGB's torture, given his knowledge, the wholesale effect on the underground Catholic Church in Eastern Europe, Lithuania, and Western Ukraine would have been immediate and catastrophic. It would have meant the wholesale collapse of the Catholic Church's efforts to nurture the flock behind the Iron Curtain. He later learned after his release from captivity that while he was imprisoned, the Roman Catholic Church in the "captive nations" of Eastern Europe functioned as normally as could be expected, given the repressive day-to-day environment of having to operate in Marxist-Leninist party-states ruthlessly adept at persecutional counterintelligence.

There's also another explanation, a thoroughly Roman Catholic mystical one, that explains Malachi Martin's survival under circumstances that reduced most prisoners to shambling zombies in body and soul. Here, necessity forces me to sequentially diverge from the late 1950s to the time that traces back to Malachi Martin's childhood in the late 1920s in the bucolic Ballylongford, County Kerry, Ireland. To my knowledge, Malachi never spoke of his mystical experiences to anyone else; if he did, they are likely no longer alive to tell of it. Malachi Martin's life, first as a Jesuit, then a Jesuit priest, then a secular cleric, was never a career or a job. It was a vocation, a calling beyond space and time from the gentle Galilean Redeemer who walked the shores of Lake Gennesaret in current-day Israel two thousand years ago.

Malachi confided to me that he was blessed as a child to experience the reality of heavenly secrets and manifestations of the Lord Jesus Christ and His Mother, the Blessed Virgin Mary. He told me on various occasions, "Before I came into the hands of my Jesuit intellectual teachers, and specifically because they very faithfully instructed me in the Church's traditional supernatural works of piety, I realized I had experienced the transcendence of the Lord Jesus's divinity through visions and locutions with exclusively supernatural meaning from my early childhood through my teens. At that early age, none of this seemed unusual or out of the ordinary; I took it for granted and presumed every other Roman Catholic had the same experience. I most often beheld the Blessed Virgin Mary under her title of Our Lady of Mount Carmel, holding the Christ Child."

Malachi consecrated his life to the Blessed Virgin Mary on July 16, 1937, on his sixteenth birthday, the feast of Our Lady of

Mount Carmel—his favorite title of the Mother of God and the one he revered with the greatest love and affection for the rest of his earthly life. Seventeen years later, on August 15, 1954, in Louvain, Belgium, the eager young Jesuit responded with a whole-hearted *"ad sum"* to the call of Holy Mother Church, inviting him to faithfully serve as one of Her priests, according to the Order of Melchizedek, until the end of his earthly days. As Leo Cardinal Suenens softly spoke the prayers of ordination and anointed the *"ordinand"* with the sacred chrism oil, the indelible character of the Sacrament was permanently imprinted upon the soul of the fervent thirty-two-year-old Malachi. Then, a most amazing event transpired. Perhaps each priest experiences a similar internal trans-formation of his soul upon his ordination; as an ordinary layman, I don't know. No one can witness the phenomenon except the newly ordained *alter Christus* (Latin for "another Christ"). The unseen Crucified Christ reached down from His Cross, grasped the young Jesuit by his hands, his feet—and most importantly, his *will*—and fastened them to His own. Henceforth and forever, the Crucified Savior communicated wordlessly that they would live their lives as One. For the rest of his time among those of us trapped in this "geophysical time grid," as Malachi put it, loneliness would never plague him again. Eternally transfixed now to Jesus, their mutual Crucifixion would be renewed each day on the altar in the Holy Sacrifice of the Roman Mass—offered to the Eternal Father for the salvation of souls and glory of the Church.

"Consummatum est," whispered the Savior into his ear.

"Fiat," replied the enraptured young priest...and Jesus smiled.

This previously hidden mystical aspect of Malachi Martin's life (he was far too self-effacing to speak at length about it with me, necessitating my having to gather it mosaic-style via countless con-versations until after seven or so years, I had my "a-ha!" moment, nor would he openly acknowledge it in a public forum), is the key to understanding his survival at the hands of the vicious KGB. While he was their prisoner, Malachi daily underwent his own version of Jesus's scourging by the brutal Roman soldiers in the Prætorium, but he received consolation specifically from his earlier childhood mystical experiences. His survival in the KGB's infamous Lviv Prison on Lontskoho bears a striking resemblance years later to the story of Josyp Terelya, the Ukrainian Uniate prisoner who was allegedly saved from freezing to death in a Soviet punishment cell by the intercession of the Blessed Virgin Mary.

Malachi told me that there were several instances when he described himself as being at the "end of his rope" due to beatings from the KGB guards or extended stays in the sloped-floor ice water cells, and he silently whispered over and over the second half of the Hail Mary prayer. As prayer was strictly forbidden, and the Soviet guards were always on the lookout for reasons to further punish prisoners, he quietly recited the prayer in his childhood Gaelic: "*A Mhuire naofa, a Mháthair Dé, guigh orainn na peacaigh anois, agus ar uair an bháis*" (Holy Mary, Mother of God, pray for us sinners now and at the hour of our death). Gaelic, of course, was completely incomprehensible to the Soviet guards, and they took his words to be the incoherent ramblings of a lunatic prisoner who had been beaten and shocked one too many times. It was during one of these episodes, confined in a sloped-floor ice water cell, that Malachi sensed the approach of death, and so he continued the recitation of the Gaelic Hail Mary as his excruciating torments increased. If imminent death was to be his lot, the young Jesuit was determined in his final moments to unite his sufferings to those of the crucified Lord to whom he had pledged himself body and soul only a few years earlier. Suddenly, an inexplicable warmth and invigoration surged through his enervated frame. He described opening his eyes to see the Virgin Mary in her classic portrayal of Our Lady of Mount Carmel. Malachi described her as wearing a gold crown, with twelve stars surrounding her head, holding the infant Jesus as a toddler perched on her arm, with both holding the brown scapular in their outstretched hands.

Malachi said he had no idea how long he stared at the vision of the Virgin and the Christ Child but remembered that he couldn't find the strength to get up from a crouching position near the water's edge. His ingrained Jesuit skepticism kicked in hard until he remembered his mystical childhood experiences in Ireland and that one of these was of the very vision he was seeing now in his prison cell: Our Lady of Mount Carmel holding the Child Jesus. Malachi said that the Virgin and Child Jesus appeared to him on three or four separate occasions during his sixteen-month imprisonment, and always when he felt he was on the brink of death. There was never any auditory or locutionary communication, just the silently reassuring presence of the Mother of God and Her infant Son, Jesus. He also described what he called the "intervention of my Guardian Angel" during the worst electrical torture sessions. There were several sessions when the KGB guards took great delight in seeing how much current his slim body could withstand from the electrical cattle prod. Although the pain was intense, Malachi said there were numerous times when by all rights he should have lost consciousness due to the pain but rather endured the voltage coursing through his body with minimal discomfort or medical trauma to either his genitals or anal area. During these interrogation punishment sessions, his internal locutions from his Guardian Angel returned to reassure him that he would suffer greatly but not die. His Guardian Angel also told the prisoner that his suffering was pleasing to God because Malachi was joining his own to that of the suffering Christ on the Cross, offering himself as a victim soul for the conversion of sinners and in reparation for sins committed against the Sacred Heart of Jesus. Jesuit priests, until recently, have historically had a great zeal for promoting devotion to the Sacred Heart of Jesus among the faithful.

Despite countless attempts to get the young Roman bishop to confess to "illegal religious activities" and "conspiring to organize counterrevolutionary elements against the U.S.S.R.," Soviet authorities could not extract a confession of any sort from Malachi Martin. Word had gotten back to the Vatican by circuitous means in early 1958 that Malachi Martin was still alive and languishing in the Ukrainian prison, the victim of hideous KGB torture. The Holy See's diplomatic corps swung into action. At the direction of an ailing Pope Pius XII, a quietly intense pressure campaign was mounted against Moscow to release the prisoner. Finally, in late May 1958, Soviet authorities in Lviv put Malachi Martin on a train to Vienna, Austria, gaunt and dressed in an ill-fitting, coarse wool suit and nothing else. Several days later, a grateful Bishop Malachi Martin knelt to kiss the Ring of the Fisherman worn by Pope Pius XII to express his gratitude. Malachi recounted to me how the pontiff, with a well-earned reputation for an icy demeanor, looked at him and said, using the royal "we" form of address, "We have prayed to Our Lord Jesus Christ for your safe return, and He has graciously heard our request. Thanks be to God."

After several weeks of medical recovery, on his return to the Vatican, his superiors assigned Malachi Martin to serve as the private secretary to the famed Augustin Cardinal Bea. Martin worked with the German Jesuit cardinal in the Vatican until 1964, almost to the conclusion of the Second Vatican Ecumenical Council.

5

ANIMUS NURTURED
BY BITTERNESS

One of Malachi's most enduring detractors (*slanderers...?*) was the late journalist Robert Blair Kaiser, who passed away in 2015, shortly after we interviewed him at a Phoenix hospice facility for the 2016 Netflix documentary about Malachi, *Hostage to the Devil*. Kaiser was a decidedly liberal progressive on all issues relating to the Catholic Church; Malachi described him as a proud Modernist. Some background is needed to understand Kaiser's multi-decade campaign of slander and *animus* towards Malachi Martin.

Robert Blair Kaiser spent ten years in formation from 1949 to 1959 to become a Jesuit priest but voluntarily left the Jesuits prior to priestly ordination to get married and take up a career as a journalist. He subsequently spent time in Rome as a correspondent for *Time* magazine covering the Second Vatican Council, where he won the Overseas Press Club's prestigious Ed Cunningham Award in 1962 for "best magazine reporting from abroad." He subsequently authored several books championing left-wing causes near and dear to American progressive Catholics. Kaiser was a persistent voice during his life for replacing the Catholic Church's hierarchic structure with a democratic "people's church." He also argued against clerical celibacy; he was in favor of ordaining women to the priesthood and permitting Catholics to use birth control. Since Modernist theology often elevates human experience over dogma, Kaiser embodied this by emphasizing the primacy of personal conscience, social justice, and structural reforms meant to diffuse authority, giving lay people the authority to choose their priests and bishops.

One Kaiser-authored book that clearly revealed his Modernist sympathies was his fictional 2011 saccharine ode to the real-life ultra-progressive Cardinal Roger Mahony of Los Angeles, entitled *Cardinal Mahony: A Novel*. It tells the story of a "fictional" American cardinal kidnapped outside his cabin in the California High Sierras by three liberation theologians. They transport him to southern Mexico in his personal helicopter and put him on trial for his sins before an international television audience. A jury of six retired Latin American bishops finds him guilty and delivers a surprising sentence. Through this experience, the bishop undergoes a pro-found religious transformation.

Having read the Amazon Kindle version, I can say that it is cringe-worthy fan fiction/hero worship, especially since Kaiser knew at the time he wrote it that Cardinal Mahony was directly implicated in the burgeoning clerical sex abuse scandal engulfing the Catholic Church in the United States. It was public knowledge; Kaiser *knew this* and wrote his cloying panegyric to Cardinal Mahony anyway. Internal Church documents released in 2013 revealed that Cardinal Mahony and top aides systematically covered up sexual abuse by priests in the Archdiocese of Los Angeles. He and his then vicar for clergy worked to shield accused priests from law enforcement by transferring them to other parishes instead of reporting them to law enforcement. Mahony also delayed or avoided cooperating with authorities investigating the sexual abuse cases, as well as advised abusive priests to avoid therapeutic counseling where they might be required to disclose their predatory actions.

It was a front-page story in the July 15, 2007, *Los Angeles Times* newspaper that the Archdiocese of Los Angeles under Cardinal Mahony agreed to pay $660 million to over five hundred victims of clergy sexual abuse; this was the largest clergy abuse settlement to date in the history of the U.S. Catholic Church. As part of the settlement, the archdiocese was forced to release thousands of internal files, exposing Mahony's direct role in covering up cases. It could be argued that, as Kaiser published his hero-worship novel several years *after* Mahony's direct role in the sordid sexual abuse scandal came to light, it shows, at a minimum, a clear bias in favor of advocating for Modernist clergy and their pet causes, even when high-ranking clerics are legally implicated in covering up heinous sex crimes.

What does this have to do with Malachi Martin? From 1965–1966 until his death in 2015, Kaiser reserved his strongest venom for Malachi Martin. In his 2002 autobiographical book, *Clerical Error: A True Story*, Kaiser directly accused Malachi Martin of having broken up his marriage by violating his priestly vows to have an affair with Kaiser's wife, Mary, while the Kaisers were in Rome for the Second Vatican Council. Kaiser's book includes as "proof" of the alleged affair the fact that both Malachi and Kaiser's soon-to-be-ex-wife, Mary, left Rome at the same time.

What is conveniently omitted here are Kaiser's struggles with mental illness and alcoholism while in Rome covering the Second Vatican Council. Malachi told me that, in desperation, Kaiser's wife, Mary, came to him during the Council about Kaiser's mental and substance abuse problems and sought assistance. A small group of Jesuits, including Malachi, and such liberal progressive Jesuit luminaries as Fr. John Courtney Murray, SJ, and Fr. Vincent O'Keefe, SJ, then staged an intervention with Kaiser over Kaiser's strident objections. Kaiser was briefly institutionalized and subsequently diagnosed with severe paranoid schizophrenia, as well as suffering from acute alcoholism. Malachi told me that Kaiser never forgave him for being one of the Jesuits who organized the intervention, and what compounded Kaiser's hatred of Malachi was that Malachi Martin, by persuading Pope Paul VI to permit Martin to leave the Jesuit order, betrayed the reformist bent of the Second Vatican Council. Frs. Murray and O'Keefe were never targets of Kaiser's venom over the mental health and alcoholism intervention; Malachi said this was because of an unspoken *dictum* Kaiser followed: *Thou shall not criticize a fellow liberal.*

Malachi also speculated that Kaiser's consistent hostility towards him emanated from Kaiser's relentless championing of senior American religious leaders who all had one thing in common: they were Modernist apostates bound together by a common hatred of Pope John Paul II and traditional Catholic teaching. Led by the late Cardinal Joseph Bernardin, the late, disgraced, ex-Cardinal Cardinal Theodore McCarrick (expelled from the priesthood in 2019 by the Vatican for his sexual abuse crimes), and Cardinal Roger Mahony, these men advanced a Modernist agenda in the American Church for decades until it was delayed by the election of Pope Benedict XVI (only to be gleefully resumed with the election of Argentine Cardinal Jorge Bergoglio in 2013). All three men were united in their hostility to Roman Catholicism as practiced before the Second Vatican Council, as well as their tolerance of or active promotion of malignant narcissism and predatory homosexuality within the ranks of the clergy. Author Randy Engel alleged Cardinal Joseph Bernardin in Chapter 15 of her 2006 book *The Rite of Sodomy: Homosexuality and the Roman Catholic Church* to have been the guiding force for many years behind what she termed the "Homosexual Collective." Malachi described it back in 1996 as a ruthlessly self-protective network of homosexual clergy who all shared two traits. First was a love of dalliances with young priests and semi-narians whom they had sexually "groomed," and second was that all of the clergy involved had everything to lose in the event they were "outed." In addition to ensuring silence, this made all like-minded clergy eminently blackmailable.

It's interesting to note that Kaiser's vitriol towards Malachi Martin lived on after his own death. In the April 3, 2015, obituary published by the heterodox publication the *National Catholic Reporter*, not only was Kaiser lionized as *"a courageous man with the biggest heart of any (church) reformer I ever met; he was dauntless in pushing, prodding and confronting injustice in the church,"* and a *"powerful force in the reform community partly because of the curmudgeonly personality with which he forcefully and unabashedly delivered his message to the world."* The obituary goes on to conveniently state as fact, without offering any objective proof, the allegation that *"the Council was a high mark in Kaiser's life, shaping it indelibly. It was also one of its darkest chapters. During those years, Kaiser and his wife hosted a friend, Jesuit Fr. Malachi Martin, who betrayed Kaiser, running off with his wife. That betrayal tortured Kaiser for many years."*

When I knew Malachi, I asked him several times why he never responded to allegations like those Kaiser and other detractors constantly leveled at him. He responded, "Rob, when people reach down to throw mud at you, it is because mud is all they have." Of course, Malachi knew all the calumnies hurled against him. However, when you look at them with dispassion (*though that's hard to do*), the slanders are all meant to do one thing. *To tear down.* They are not critiques of Malachi's thoughts, his writing, or revelations about corruption in high places in the Church he loved and lived for. To think that Malachi's accusers are out for him alone would be a gross mistake. In this case, the intent is not just to kill the messenger but the message. Ultimately, to kill *the* Message.

It bears repeating the supremely important fact that Malachi Martin never responded to his detractors in kind. He never stooped to attack others and never sought revenge. He knew better than most that some of it sticks when mud is slung at you. Nevertheless, Malachi never let vanity, pride, or wounded feelings distract him from his apostolate, from his unceasing work for God and for His true Vicar and His true Church. The object of his detractors was always to tear down. Malachi Martin's objective was and remains (through his works) to build up our understanding, faith, and courage. To help us face the dissolution of Rome's manifestly corrupted ecclesiastical structures—the "accidental" chanceries and offices, the bricks-and-mortar housing of the Church. Malachi intended to help us see that it is Our Lord Himself, the Lord of history, who is doing that, and to see that, loving Lord that He is, Jesus will build a new and far superior housing for His ecclesial Church. The indefectible Church He founded on Peter. That is the point of every book Malachi Martin wrote. From clear-eyed analyses to painfully accurate revelations and prophecies in *The Keys of This Blood* and *Windswept House*. When you come down to it, one of the problems for Malachi Martin's gossiping detractors is that *they can't destroy his body of work, so the effort must be to destroy Malachi himself.*

I think Robert Blair Kaiser was a man whose sharp-edged ego wouldn't permit him to admit personal responsibility for the deep failures in his own life: his career, his marriage, and even his failed "stay" in a mental institution. The main point of his autobiography, *Clerical Error*, is to defame Malachi Martin and accuse him of immoral behavior and responsibility for the shambles of Kaiser's life. Of course, Kaiser could have made these accusations any time before 1999, while Malachi was still alive. It is the mark of supreme cowardice that Kaiser waited until his victim was no longer here to defend himself—which is to say, until Kaiser could no longer be sued for libel. As he revealed in *Clerical Error*, Kaiser lived a life marinated in bitterness, and with this book, he came to dance a bitter dance on the grave of a great priest.

Was Malachi Martin a sinner? I would ask the reader, *Are you?* Am I? I can only answer for myself. *I am.* My greatest comfort as a sinner? Let me borrow a reminder from Father Perricone, the great priest who introduced me to Malachi Martin. Had a sign been posted at the outer boundaries of Calvary on that first Good Friday where the Man-God Jesus hung slowly asphyxiating on the Roman death gibbet, it would have read, *"Only sinners enter here."* For Jesus came pointedly and only for us. For us sinners. Even for the vicious, wagging tongues...

6

LOVER OR LANDLADY?

Once Malachi Martin established his reputation in the 1970s as a controversial Catholic author and defender of traditional orthodox Roman Catholicism, his detractors, without hard evidence, began to circulate vicious rumors about the nature of his relationship with his landlady, Kakia Livanos. Kakia was the aristocratically sharp widow of a wealthy Greek shipping magnate, George M. Livanos, a contemporary and associate of another renowned Greek shipping industrialist, Aristotle Onassis (whom Jacqueline Kennedy married after her husband, President John F. Kennedy, was assassinated). After being invited to Malachi's residence on East 63rd Street, where I met Mrs. Livanos, their platonic relationship quickly became apparent. It took Kakia a good year to warm up to my presence in Malachi's life. It wasn't until Malachi told her that she could trust me implicitly that Mrs. Livanos began to warm up to me.

Kakia Livanos was an accomplished artist specializing in the form of painting popularized by the late Isabel O'Neil at her world-famous Isabel O'Neil Studio in New York City; she was an acclaimed authority in the decorative arts and the art of the painted finish. Admirers of Isabel's work persuaded her to teach, and in 1955, she founded her renowned studio workshop in New York City. In Europe, Isabel discovered the method of instruction she used as a model for her school: the guild system of the Renaissance. In this system, novice students learn through apprenticing under master craftsmen. Skilled apprentices, in turn, instruct new students. This method of teaching and adherence to the recommended curriculum ensures that every student has the same training and that each student understands and maintains the exacting standards of the Studio.

One of her earliest and most prolific students was Kakia Livanos. The first few times I visited Malachi in the Livanos residence, I was struck by the sheer number of artworks lovingly created by the hand of Kakia Livanos; the walls of the family apartment complex were literally *covered* in them. In 1996, Kakia presented me with a 12" x 20" bas-relief of medieval cherubs painted in her signature style. Although she might never admit it, Malachi told me it was Kakia's way of welcoming me into her extended family, as he was adamant that only a select few ever received such a gift from Kakia. The family's trust in me was further cemented the following summer when Mrs. Livanos's daughter Genie Fuhrmann's pet dog passed away. She couldn't bear the thought of burying him in an animal cemetery, and she had heard Malachi wax poetic about my family's home in suburban New Jersey, especially with my brother Kenny's passion for gardening. So, the request was made through Malachi: Would my family consider letting her bury her dog's ashes in my parents' spacious suburban yard? Of course, the answer was yes, and Genie Fuhrmann's beloved dog still rests there under a verdant canopy of oak and maple trees.

Does any of this prove Malachi Martin did not have an inappropriate relationship with Kakia Livanos? No, as any student of elementary logic knows, it's impossible to prove a negative. Am I convinced that there was nothing else between them other than the platonic friendship described above? Without a doubt. To accuse

Malachi Martin of engaging in a sordid affair smears and slanders the memory of two great people.

Americans are mostly unfamiliar with the old European practice of the wealthy, especially aristocratic families, "adopting" a priest as a personal, live-in spiritual advisor. Such priests routinely became *de facto* members of the family. A precedent that many Americans are familiar with would be the situation of the famous von Trapp Family Singers, made famous in the movie *The Sound of Music*. The von Trapp Family Singers adopted Msgr. Franz Mathias Wasner as their in-house family priest in Austria beginning in 1935.

Father Franz Mathias Wasner graduated in theology from the University of Innsbruck. After he completed his academic studies, Wasner was ordained a priest on March 17, 1929, and served in the small parish of Mayrhofen in the Tyrol region of Austria for one year. Then, much like Malachi, he went to Rome to study ecclesiastical law and graduated *summa cum laude* in 1934. Father Wasner then returned to Salzburg to serve as a priest, where he subsequently met Georg von Trapp, the patriarch of the soon-to-be-famous Trapp Family Singers. The two men formed a lifelong friendship that soon extended to the entire family. He heard the family sing on an initial visit to the von Trapp household. A highly accomplished musician, Father Wasner began to help the family with their music and discovered that their musical talent could provide them with a viable income. Father Wasner became the family's musical director and conductor for over twenty years. They initially toured as the Trapp Family Choir (later the Trapp Family Singers), performing around Europe and America. When the von Trapps left Austria in 1938, he went with them to the U.S. and lived with the family as their live-in spiritual advisor, conductor, composer, and arranger until 1958. Msgr. Wasner was so much a part of their family that he fled with the von Trapps to the U.S. after the Nazis sought to draft

Baron von Trapp as a U-Boat commander in Hitler's navy, the Nazi *Kriegsmarine*. Father Wasner was omitted from the Hollywood version of the von Trapp family's life, *The Sound of Music*, but he was buried in their family plot in Stowe, Vermont, after he died in 1992.

Unlike Father Wasner, Malachi's enemies, including certain high-ranking Jesuits, ensured that a gossip and rumor machine went into high gear peddling the lie that he was having a romantic affair with Kakia Livanos. Again, Father Martin's relationship with this woman was exclusively platonic. As previously mentioned, people in the United States are unable to relate to this practice of having an "adopted" family priest as very few well-to-do Catholic families in the USA ever have such a spiritual advisor. Although the family was Greek Orthodox, they took to Malachi as one of their own. Kakia took it upon herself to serve as Malachi's gatekeeper, as Malachi himself, in his desire to help souls, would often give out his address and telephone number in his appearances on media outlets such as *The Art Bell Show*.

If I could discern anything resembling a relationship between Kakia and Malachi, it was that she fiercely protected him from the eyes of a prying public with a motherly solicitude. As Malachi suffered from a medical condition known as heart arrhythmia, dating back to his torture at the hands of the KGB, Mrs. Livanos also became Malachi's self-appointed dietary watchdog as well. Any food that might contribute to his cholesterol levels and potentially aggravate his heart condition was strictly forbidden in the residence. Malachi subsequently took great glee in stealing away to our favorite "greasy spoon diner" on Lexington Avenue, where our standing order was a three-egg plain omelet for him, a turkey club sandwich on rye for me, and a mountain of well-done French fries between the two of us to share.

7

WINDING THE DOOMSDAY CLOCK: THE THIRD SECRET OF FATIMA

During his lifetime over the course of many interviews with Bernard Janzen of Triumph Communications, as well as Art Bell's *Coast to Coast AM* syndicated radio program, Malachi revealed select details surrounding one of the most controversial Catholic texts of our times—The Third Secret of Fatima—that ran *counter* to the narrative in the controversial (some say incomplete or *fake*) version published in 2000 by the Vatican after Malachi's death. The eldest of the three young seers, Lucia, told her bishop during World War II that the Virgin and Jesus had given her strict instructions for the pope to read and publicly reveal the Secret's text in 1960. Under the conditions of the Pontifical Secret (wherein he couldn't reveal the contents of the Third Secret unless explicitly authorized by the pope), Malachi was permitted to read a translation of the entire document, which outlines *"the end of these Catholic times,"* if the mandate of the Mother of Christ and Queen of Heaven was ignored.

Some brief background is in order here, but the events surrounding the appearance of Our Lady of Fatima are well documented in many famous books. In a part of the small village of Fatima, Portugal, called the *Cova da Iria*, the Virgin Mary appeared to three young shepherd children: Lucia dos Santos and her younger cousins, Francisco and Jacinta Marto, beginning on May 13, 1917, and continuing for six months until October 13th. These were not the first supernatural encounters the young Fatima shepherds experienced. Starting in April 1916 and continuing through the summer until mid-autumn 1916, the three children were visited by a separate heavenly apparition that identified itself alternately as "the Angel of Peace" and "the Guardian Angel of Portugal." In addition to telling the children that they need not fear him, the angel also urged them to offer prayers and sacrifices to God as reparation for sin. He taught them to recite a special prayer:

> *"My God, I believe, I adore, I hope, and I love You. I ask pardon for those who do not believe, do not adore, do not hope, and do not love You."*

The angel appeared to the children three times to prepare them for the forthcoming apparitions of the Virgin Mary. The Virgin first appeared to the children on May 13th, 1917. The children described her as being brighter than the sun, dressed in a white mantle, and holding a rosary. The Virgin told them to devote themselves to worshipping the Holy Trinity and pray the Rosary daily for World War I to end. During the monthly visitations of the Blessed Virgin Mary, she revealed to the children the reality of Hell, the approach of World War II during the reign of Pope Pius XI, and a later warning to Lucia that if Russia was not specifically consecrated to Her Immaculate Heart, it would spread its errors around the World.

In her final appearance in October 1917, the Virgin revealed herself as "the Lady of the Rosary" and announced that World War I would end. The seventy thousand plus onlookers then described a phenomenon known as the "great miracle of the sun," whereby the sun appeared to transform into a spinning disc that radiated resplendent colors and seemed to fall towards the earth. Many onlookers fell to their knees, convinced it was the end of the world. After a few terrifying minutes, the sun resumed its normal place in the sky. This phenomenon was visible to tens of thousands of people gathered in Fatima: believers, agnostics, and atheists alike.

A key part of the Virgin of Fatima's appearance became known as the "Three Secrets" entrusted to the young shepherd children. The first secret consisted of the Virgin showing the young seers an actual vision of Hell, with unrepentant souls being tormented. The second secret was that World War I would shortly end, but that if humanity did not stop offending God, a far worse war would break out during Pope Pius XI's reign. "If men do not refrain from offending God, another and far more terrible war will begin during the pontificate of Pius XI. When you see *a night that is lit by a strange and unknown light* (emphasis added), you will know it is the sign God gives you that He is about to punish the world with war and with hunger and by the persecution of the Church and the Holy Father."[2]

Twenty years later, on the night of the January 25–26, 1938, from 9 p.m. until 2 a.m., the Northern Hemisphere sky was aflame with a strange red glow and a crackling noise that to this day scientists have still not been able to explain credibly—not even as an especially intense display of the aurora borealis. It was witnessed in most of Europe, from Norway to Gibraltar, from Portugal to Greece, and as far south as North Africa and the continental United States. Panicky New Yorkers pulled dozens of Manhattan

---

1. (Author's note: The Virgin told the young shepherd children the papal name the successor to then reigning Pope Benedict XV, Cardinal Achille Ratti, would take upon his election to the papacy five years in the future in the conclave that ended on February 6, 1922. There is no way the poor, illiterate shepherd children of Fatima could have known Cardinal Ratti would be elected as the future pope in 1922, much less take the name "Pius XI.")

fire alarm boxes, thinking the Bronx was on fire. Gazing at the sky with his top Nazi advisors on his private hideaway's veranda near Berchtesgaden, Germany, Adolf Hitler saw this strange red light in the sky as a sign from his own dark occult gods and announced: "To this point, we have avoided violence to obtain Lebensraum; now we must shed blood...."

The final and most controversial secret has gained notoriety as "The Third Secret of Fatima." It was written down by now Sister Lucia in her Portugal convent under the direct order of her bishop in 1944. Sister Lucia had such trouble putting pen to paper that it was only after receiving the permission of the Virgin Mary to write it down in obedience to her bishop that Sister Lucia could do so. At the time, all that was known of the Third Secret were the introductory words of the Virgin Mary: "In Portugal, the dogma of the Faith will always be preserved..."

Sister Lucia said the Third Secret was to be released no later than 1960, as its meaning would be clearer then; however, 1960 came and went with only a terse message from the Vatican Press Office that the Vatican would not publish the message. There are many exhaustive, famous treatments of the apparitions of Our Lady of Fatima, and my intent here is to only touch on the highlights. The additional words of the Virgin after the enigmatic mention of Portugal and the ellipsis have never been made known, despite the Third Secret allegedly being revealed by the Vatican in 2000 by Cardinal Sodano. Instead, the Vatican described a vision of a "bishop in white" ascending a mountain over the corpses of dead faithful, where he is killed at the summit by soldiers shooting arrows and bullets, along with the fiery punishment of Earth by an angel brandishing a flaming spear being stopped by the hand of the Virgin. The Vatican would go on to claim that the Third Secret was a prophecy of the attempted assassination of Pope John Paul II by a Turkish gunman in St. Peter's Square. As he died in July 1999, Malachi Martin was never privy to this Vatican version published a year later. He did tell me that if the Vatican ever released a version of the Third Secret that was false or altered, he would have taken out a full-page article in the *New York Times* denouncing the fraud and revealing the actual Third Secret.

Here is where the controversy starts. Malachi told me that in February 1960, he was summoned by his Jesuit superior, Augustin Cardinal Bea, early one morning to accompany his eminence to a meeting at the papal apartments in the Vatican. The two clerics entered the Apostolic Palace, but Malachi told me that he was bid to wait in an antechamber while Cardinal Bea entered Pope John XXIII's apartment, along with several other high-ranking clergy. Malachi described to me how, over the course of the following hour, he heard arguments inside that meeting that rose to the level of shouting. It culminated in a visibly irate Cardinal Bea brusquely storming out of the papal apartments, only acknowledging Malachi's presence with a curt *"Malachi, lass uns gehen!!! (Malachi, let's go!!!)"* The two Jesuits got into the back of Cardinal Bea's waiting car, and as they settled into their seats, Malachi related how Bea muttered aloud, "Those fools have just condemned millions upon millions of people to a horrible fate."

When Malachi inquired about the Cardinal's cryptic statement, he said Cardinal Bea withdrew an envelope with a German translation of the Third Secret. Before handing it over to the young Bishop (*in pectore*) Martin, Cardinal Bea made Malachi swear an oath that he would never divulge the precise contents of the Secret unless permitted to do so by the pope himself. Malachi readily consented to the papal oath and read the Third Secret in the back of Cardinal Bea's car before handing the letter back to his boss.

Of course, this account only served to whet my appetite regarding the letter's contents. Malachi never told me the precise contents, only speaking of them in roundabout terms. He did say that one key part concerned a great apostasy, or loss of true faith, in the Roman Catholic Church and that this apostasy would originate "from the very top of the Church." Cardinal Mario Ciappi, papal theologian to the five popes stretching from Pope Pius XII to Pope John Paul II, subsequently echoed this dire waning using almost the same precise phraseology. The implication is that "from the very top of the Church" means the papacy. I asked Malachi if this meant that the Devil would possess a future pope. Malachi shook his head vehemently, indicating no. He said that Lucifer could "control" a pope without such a pope being formally possessed. Malachi also said the letter made a short but precise reference to an undiscovered source of limitless free energy. This intriguing tidbit is perhaps why the Soviet KGB tried multiple times to steal the Third Secret from the papal apartments.

When I asked him what Cardinal Bea meant when he alluded to the deaths of millions of people, Malachi told me to look up what Pope John Paul II told a group of pilgrims during a visit to Fulda, Germany, in 1980. As a former Soviet/Warsaw Pact military analyst for the CIA, Fulda, Germany, immediately resonated with me. As it was known, the "Fulda Gap" was the strategic location on the border between East and West Germany where the elite Category A assault divisions of the Soviet 8th Guards Army and the 1st Guards Tank Army faced off against the U.S. Army V Corps. Most U.S. and NATO war planners acknowledged the landscape as one of the most likely routes for a massive Soviet thrust into West Germany towards the Rhine River outside of the North German Plain, due to the suitability of its terrain to maneuver warfare. It was considered an ideal invasion route for the Soviets and their allied Warsaw Pact follow-on forces if and when they invaded Western Europe.

According to the October 1981 issue of the West German publication *Stimme des Glaubens* (*The Time of the Believers*), the Holy Father was asked by a group of devout pilgrims, "What about the Third Secret of Fatima? Should it not have already been published by 1960?" Pope John Paul II replied: "Given the seriousness of the contents, my predecessors in the Petrine office have diplomatically preferred to postpone publication to not encourage the world power of Communism to make certain moves.

"On the other hand, it should be sufficient for all Christians to know this: *if there is a message in which it is written that the oceans will flood whole areas of the earth and that from one moment to the next, millions of people will perish,* truly the publication of such a message is no longer something to be so much desired." The pope continued: "Many wish to know simply from curiosity and a taste for the sensational, but they forget that knowledge also implies responsibility. They only seek the satisfaction of their curiosity, and that is dangerous if at the same time, they are not disposed to do something and if they are convinced that it is impossible to do anything against evil."

At this point, the pope grasped his rosary and said: "Here is the remedy against this evil. Pray, pray, and ask for nothing more. Leave everything else to the Mother of God."

The Holy Father was then asked: "What is going to happen to the Church?"

John Paul II answered: "We must prepare ourselves to suffer great trials before long, such as will demand of us a disposition to give up even life, and a total dedication to Christ and for Christ.... With your and my prayers, it is possible to mitigate this tribulation, but it is no longer possible to avert it because only thus can the Church be effectively renewed. How many times has the renewal of the Church sprung from blood? This time, too, it will not be otherwise. We must be strong and prepared, and trust in Christ and His Mother, and be very, very assiduous in praying the Rosary."

After researching this information, the next time we sat down for lunch, I asked Malachi if what the pope had said at Fulda in the Autumn of 1980 was an accurate representation of the hidden secret when John Paul II said, *"The oceans will flood whole areas of the earth, and that from one moment to the next millions of people will perish...."* He only gave me a piercing stare in response.

It seems that, despite saying that the Holy See preferred to withhold the Third Secret to avoid sensational exploitation, His Holiness then proceeded to speak precisely of great floods, millions of people perishing, and a bloody persecution of the Catholic Church in the not-too-distant future. In the parlance of the current day in 2025, it could be argued that Pope John Paul II "said the quiet part out loud." Malachi also added to this when he said, "Rob, how do you think people would react if the Vatican released such a message? A message that also spoke of a violent, apocalyptic darkness covering the earth for three straight days, like one of the plagues visited on the Pharoah for defying Moses?"

Pope John Paul II's words to the pilgrims at Fulda are in marked contrast to the "official" Third Secret released by the Vatican in 2000. John Paul II spoke of future events, but the Vatican contradicted itself in 2000 by insisting Fatima's Third Secret belonged to the past. In my opinion, I have no doubt one reason the Vatican chose to release its "version" in 2000 was that Malachi Martin had died a year earlier and there was no one else alive who had made such a direct threat to call out the Holy See for lying by taking out a full-page ad in the *New York Times*. Given his prominence, had Malachi Martin made good on his threat to publicly reveal the true Third Secret, it would have given the Vatican a geopolitical migraine headache, calling into doubt the credibility of senior Vatican hierarchy, right up to the pope himself. In the twenty-six years since Malachi's death and the Vatican's official pronouncement on Fatima, the controversy over the actual contents of Sister Lucia's 1944 letter has only grown sharper, especially during the controversial pontificate of the late Pope Francis.

8

THE GATES OF HELL
SHALL NOT PREVAIL

When the United States and Soviet Union almost came to blows during the 1962 Cuban missile crisis, the Vatican already had in place a plan to keep the worldwide Roman Church alive in the event of a global nuclear holocaust. Although we were close friends, being aware that I was a CIA operations officer, it's not that he was guarded in what he told me, it's just that Malachi exercised a necessary degree of prudence in our discussions, given his station. One such episode concerns the existential threat posed to the worldwide Roman Catholic Church by the Soviet Union in the wake of the Second World War. Following the death of Joseph Stalin in 1953, the mantle of leadership as first secretary of the Communist Party of the Soviet Union (CPSU) came to rest on the shoulders of Nikita Khrushchev. Many people assume that Stalin was the greatest enemy of religion in the Soviet Union and the captive satellite nations of Eastern Europe, but this was not the case. Some of the most ruthless persecution of religious believers took place upon Khrushchev's ascension to power, and given his own encounter with the Soviet secret police in the 1950s, Malachi Martin knew firsthand the existential threat the Russia-centric Marxist-Leninist party state posed. Whereas Stalin sarcastically asked, "How many divisions has the pope got...?" his successor wasn't taking any chances. Not only was the new Soviet dictator more repressive towards religious belief than his predecessor, but he was also more bellicose. This was highlighted by episodes such as Khrushchev's infamous speech before a group of Western ambassadors at the Polish embassy in Moscow in 1956, where he uttered his infamous phrase, "We will bury you."

Modern historians have ascribed a more nuanced view to Khrushchev's bluster. They believe he was referring to the inevitable triumph of the Marxist-Leninist party state's socialism over the liberal Western democracies. Political leaders in the West at the time and the Vatican of Pope Pius XII took the new CPSU chairman's statement at face value. Although it now seems like distant history, the geopolitical situation of the 1950s and early 1960s was much more black and white than our current multipolar world would suggest. Whereas the Western allies, for example, the United States, Great Britain, and France, rapidly demobilized their respective armies after World War II upon the defeat of Nazi Germany, this was not the case with the Soviet Union. The Soviet Red Army maintained an army of over one million troops in Eastern Europe to ensure the political dominance of local communist puppet regimes in lockstep with Moscow's dictates. The world watched a demonstration of this during the abortive 1956 Hungarian Revolution, where the Soviet Red Army ruthlessly crushed an uprising by Hungarian freedom fighters.

Given the objectively real threat that the Red Army posed to Western Europe, and backed up by the Soviets' growing nuclear weapons arsenal, Malachi told me the Vatican of Pope Pius XII was under no illusions about the threat Khrushchev's militant Soviet Union represented. It wasn't just the internal Soviet persecution of the underground Roman Catholic Church that Malachi himself experienced firsthand. For the first time in history, a malignant geopolitical state actor had the capability, and perhaps the intent, to turn Vatican City State and the rest of the Eternal City into an irradiated nuclear hellscape. Pragmatist that Pope Pius XII was, he foresaw the critical need for the worldwide governance structures of the Roman Church to continue should such destruction occur.

To facilitate the continuity of the Holy See, Malachi said that Pope Pius XII chose twelve cardinals in consultation with his closest advisors, who were already in place in strategic locations worldwide. Malachi described these locations as "the twelve administrative regions," euphemistically chosen after the Twelve Apostles. These regions would be governed by one of Pius's chosen cardinals to ensure the continued function of the global Roman Church in the event of nuclear war. This was Pope Pius's practical application of the words of Jesus in Matthew 16:18: *"And I say unto thee: that thus art Peter; and upon this rock I will build my church, and the gates of hell shall not prevail against it."* In the eyes of Pope Pius XII, the Soviet Union and its communist allies around the globe certainly represented the "gates of Hell." This also directly refers to the dire warning the Virgin Mary gave the shepherd children at Fatima on July 13, 1917: "If my requests are heeded, Russia will be converted, and there will be peace. If not, she will spread her errors throughout the world, causing wars and persecution of the Church. The good will be martyred, the Holy Father will have much to suffer, ***and various nations will be annihilated.***" Pope Pius XII saw this message from the Virgin Mary as Heaven's direct insertion of itself into human geopolitical affairs, and he acted on the dire "or else" posed by the Mother of Christ. Pius XII was a pragmatist, and he knew that humanity had not followed the Virgin's calls at Fatima to cease offending her Son. He knew in his heart that already the captive nations of Eastern Europe had been "annihilated" so far as their personal and religious freedoms were concerned.

I became privy to this information during the late 1990s when Malachi asked me to drive him to Dr. Rama Coomaraswamy's residence in Wilton, Connecticut, for Coomaraswamy's successive ordinations to the Roman Catholic diaconate and then ordination as a Catholic priest. The Coomaraswamy family had recently moved from their home in Stamford, Connecticut, to Wilton and was still unpacking, so the house was still in a state of chaos. Several ordaining clergy had traveled some distance to officiate at the ceremony, and Malachi asked me to drive him up to Wilton.

On the way back to Manhattan after the ordination (and I am dimly visible as one of the figures in attendance in extant Internet photos of the ordination service), Malachi and I were chatting when in an apparent spontaneous bit of anger (but which I later learned was quite deliberate), Malachi turned to me and said "You know, Rob, Rama pestered me for months to have a cardinal from the Vatican present at his ordination, and when I finally agreed, he didn't even have the civility to offer me so much as a damn cup of coffee...." As I was driving my Jeep down the winding back roads of Connecticut at the time, I resisted the temptation to swerve off the road and could only glance at Malachi with an inquiring look. Later, when we were back having coffee at the Livanos apartment, I broached the topic of "the cardinal from the Vatican" whom Malachi had referenced. Malachi said that after his *in pectore* elevation to the episcopate during the reign of Pius XII, he was elevated, also in secret, to the rank of cardinal. When I asked why, Malachi told me very matter-of-factly that he was the senior representative of the *Servizio Privato* for the United States and Canada.

He explained that the *Servizio* was a small, elite intelligence service, answerable only to the pope in Rome. He acknowledged his role as *de facto* head of Vatican Intelligence in the United States, and if there was a nuclear war between the United States and the Soviet Union, provided he survived a nuclear exchange, he was one of the twelve apostolic administrators charged with overseeing the continued functioning of the Roman Catholic Church in the United States until a conclave could be held to elect a new pope. When I asked Malachi why he chose to disclose this to me, as he knew I was a recently retired CIA officer, he gave me a piercing stare down his reading glasses and said, "Because I trust you to keep your mouth shut," and I did for the better part of thirty years. This book is the first instance where I am publicly divulging Malachi's status as a cardinal, as Malachi's death in July 1999 released me from my promise to keep this knowledge confidential. Will the Vatican ever acknowledge this? My guess is that Hell will freeze over first. I surmise outright denial or accusations of fabrication against this author are much more likely, especially given the Modernist winds prevailing in the Vatican.

9

THE DEVIL INFILTRATES
THE VATICAN

Malachi wrote the 1996 "factional" bestseller *Windswept House*, which recalled a Satanic ceremony performed in the Vatican's Pauline Chapel on the night of June 30–July 1, 1963. Malachi said that the malign ceremony came to light over ten years after it happened when one of the participants confessed on his deathbed to having taken part. The priest who was hearing the shocking confession conditioned absolution of the dying penitent on the confessor revealing the sordid episode's details to higher authorities within the Vatican. Just as the old saying goes that "there are no atheists in foxholes," Malachi told me that the dying penitent found himself peering over the edge of the abyss of death into the very real possibility of eternal damnation in Hell for his role in the black mass and was craving absolution. Malachi explained to me that, although *Windswept House* in its entirety was a "factional" book, he was subsequently able to glean enough details from his confidential contacts in the Vatican to convince him 1963's purported evil event was true.

When I asked why he didn't just name those involved in the evil rite, Malachi quipped, "Because I want to keep my kneecaps." The so-called enthronement, or black mass, was conducted in the Vatican's Pauline Chapel along with a simultaneous corresponding ceremony in South Carolina in the United States, with the respective malignant actors in real-time contact over a transatlantic telephone line. The evil ceremony inside the Vatican (which Luciferians refer to as "The Citadel of the High Enemy") allegedly gave the Fallen Angel a strong spiritual and temporal foothold in the Vatican, and according to the beliefs of the Satanists, evicting the holy influence of the Lord Jesus. As previously mentioned, in the Gospel, according to Mark 16:18, Jesus Christ promised the Apostles that the gates of Hell would not prevail against his Church. Were the followers of the Fallen Angel to succeed in their malign intent, then the words of Christ would have been proven false. Malachi was at pains to emphasize that Lucifer's malign influence would extend through the Roman Catholic Church *only* to those consecrated souls who had decided to betray their vows before Christ in service to Lucifer. To wit, the power and control gained due to this enthronement would affect those corrupted souls that formed the *bureaucratic administrative hierarchy* of the Roman Catholic Church. This entailed everything from Vatican dicasteries in Rome to the smallest, most far-flung diocesan chanceries worldwide, with the only condition being that the key personalities involved, the Servitors of the Prince, as Malachi called them, had sworn unswerving dedication to Lucifer.

As any Catholic who paid attention in religion class knows, the bureaucracy of the Church and the myriad of clerical functionaries who populate it do not constitute the Roman Catholic Church. The church Jesus referred to in Mark's gospel is properly referred to as the "Mystical Body of Christ." This is a trifurcated way of referring to the three classes of membership in the Church. First is the *Church Triumphant*, those souls who have died in the state of sanctifying grace and cleansed of all attachment to sin, such that they are enjoying the Beatific Vision, the supreme bliss of contemplating the Face of God in eternity. The second group is the *Church Suffering*, or those souls who died in the state of grace but are being cleansed of any remaining residual attachment to sin in the purifying fires of Christ's love through a mysterious process known as Purgatory. Finally, there are hundreds of millions of Catholic souls still alive on Earth working out their salvation through patient lives of fidelity to Christ; this is known as the *Church Militant. This* is the Church that Jesus promised the gates of Hell would not prevail against, not local chancery offices.

On June 29, 1972, Pope Paul VI uttered his controversial public declaration, "…We would say that through some mysterious fissure—no, it's not mysterious; through some fissure, the smoke of Satan has entered the Church of God." Malachi told me how this 1963 malign ceremony frustrated Pope John Paul II's efforts in the spiritual and temporal governance of the Roman Catholic Church twenty years later. Due to the implosion of the Catholic Church that Pope Paul VI originally lamented in 1972, Malachi believed orthodox-believing Roman Catholics would need to form an "underground church" true to the pre-1962 dogmatic beliefs and ritual practices of the Roman Catholic Church.

Malachi attributed a large portion of the collapse of authentic Roman Catholicism worldwide to this "enthronement." According to the Center for Applied Research in the Apostolate (CARA), and the Gallup polling organization, statistically, there has been a wholesale collapse in both Roman Catholic belief and practice since the end of the Second Vatican Council in 1965. In addition to the tens of thousands of priests who have abandoned their vocations, along with lay brothers and nuns, according to an August 5, 2019, article by Gregory A. Smith, senior associate director of research at the Pew Research Center, 69 percent of Roman Catholics who attend weekly Mass reject the foundational dogma that Holy Communion, also known as the Blessed Sacrament, is the actual Body, Blood,

Soul, and Divinity of Jesus. Rejecting transubstantiation, where the substance of the bread and wine are truly changed into the Real Presence of Jesus Christ, they instead believe Christ's presence is merely symbolic, much in the same vein as that believed by Protestant denominations. According to an April 2024 Pew Research Study, only 28 percent of U.S. Roman Catholics attend Mass weekly. Considering the figures cited in the preceding 2019 article about belief in the Real Presence of Jesus by Greg Smith, it is apparent that a vanishingly small number of American Roman Catholics truly believe what the Church has taught for centuries.

Father Brian Harrison, a distinguished priest who also became a good friend of Malachi in the final decade of Martin's life, also lent credence and corroborated Malachi's account of the blasphemous 1963 ceremony in the Pauline Chapel in an article in the May 3, 2021, issue of the Catholic periodical *The Remnant* entitled: "The 1963 Vatican Enthronement of Lucifer: A *'Windswept House'* Update." Father Harrison, O.S., M.A., S.T.D., a retired priest of the Society of the Oblates of Wisdom, is also retired associate professor of Theology of the Pontifical Catholic University of Puerto Rico in Ponce, P.R. In 1997, he gained his doctorate in Systematic Theology, *summa cum laude*, from the *Pontifical Athenæum of the Holy Cross* in Rome, so Father Harrison's theological credentials for proffering his insights into this controversy are impeccable. Before the March 22, 2021, prohibition against private Masses being offered at the multitude of side altars and chapels inside Saint Peter's Basilica, Father Harrison was also one of the myriad priests who said daily Mass there while attending the *Athenæum* for his doctorate.

In 1996, Father Harrison had the inspired idea to offer a liturgical reparation for this blasphemous act performed decades earlier, and as he was by now a close friend of Malachi, he proposed to Malachi that they each offer the Holy Sacrifice of the Mass to this end. Malachi enthusiastically agreed that this should take place on the thirty-third anniversary of the Luciferian desecration of the Pauline Chapel. The number thirty-three is special for Roman Catholics and Luciferian Freemasons. For Catholics, according to the Bible, Jesus Christ spent thirty-three years as a man here on Earth. For Freemasons, the Thirty-Three Degrees of Freemasonry are an unacknowledged mockery of the social kingship of Christ. This teaching of the Catholic faith was formally defined in the 1923 papal encyclical by Pope Pius XI, *Quas Primas*, or *"On the Kingship of Christ."* This is rooted in the words of Christ found in Matthew 28:18, *"And Jesus coming, spoke to them, saying: All power is given to me in heaven and in earth."*

Father Harrison offered Mass in the *Novus Ordo* form of the rite (in other words, the post-Vatican II form of the Mass), and Malachi offered a corresponding Mass in the pre-1962 Traditional Latin Mass (sometimes referred to as the "Tridentine Mass," as its norms, rubrics, and prayers were codified at the sixteenth-century Council of Trent). I offer this snippet of information as corroboration that Malachi persuaded a distinguished, highly respected fellow priest that the evil ceremony *had*, in fact, taken place inside the Vatican thirty-three years earlier. Both Father Harrison and I, knowing Malachi's unswerving commitment to Christ, are convinced that Malachi would never have concocted an event such as the 1963 Luciferian Enthronement as a fictional but lurid device to increase sales of his final novel, *Windswept House*. It would be mortally sinful to concoct a fictional tale and then offer a sacred Mass intention for it. Malachi Martin was already a bestselling author and had no reason to fabricate such an outlandish tale.

For those who maintain that the 1963 Black Mass and concomitant sexual abuse of the young victim in South Carolina described in *Windswept House*, known only by the pseudonym 'Agnes', is a fanciful product of Malachi Martin's imagination, I would direct them to the recent, similarly disturbing case of Rachel Mastrogiacomo. In 2010, Rachel was in Rome discerning her vocation as a twenty-four-year-old single woman, where she was befriended by an American priest, Father Jacob Bertrand. Bertrand was ordained in 2010, assigned to the Diocese of San Diego, California, and studied in Rome when Mastrogiacomo was there. After an extended period of what sexual abuse experts refer to as 'grooming,' Father Bertrand then proceeded to ritually defile Rachel during a series of perverted masses at a private residence in Minnesota; rituals that Mastrogiacomo was subsequently informed constituted "satanic ritual sexual abuse." Her claims have been detailed in various interviews and articles, including an episode of *The Dr. J Show* hosted by the Ruth Institute (episode 146) on YouTube.

In 2014, Mastrogiacomo formally reported to the Diocese of San Diego that she had been sexually assaulted in 2010 by Father Jacob Bertrand, now the associate pastor at St. John the Evangelist Catholic Church in San Diego. Rachel reported the satanic ritual sexual abuse to then San Diego Bishop, now Cardinal of Washington, DC, Robert McElroy. McElroy is a well-known ultra-progressive cleric with a public track record of championing heterodox causes within the Church in defiance of settled Catholic dogmatic teaching. The report was submitted to McElroy via John Pendergrass, the Director of Child and Youth Protection for the Diocese of Raleigh, North Carolina, where Mastrogiacomo lived at the time. Pendergrass sent the detailed account of the abuse to the Diocese of San Diego, where it was received by Msgr. Steven Callahan, who was serving as the apostolic administrator for the Diocese of San Diego, following the death of Bishop Cirilo Flores.

According to Mastrogiacomo, Callahan presented the report to Bertrand, who admitted his guilt in Msgr. Callahan's presence. Despite

Bertrand's admission, Mastrogiacomo stated that Bishop McElroy did not take immediate or adequate action, instead leaving Father Bertrand in active ministry. She reported that neither McElroy nor the Diocese of San Diego contacted her for further information or support, and she later discovered that other complaints against Bertrand had been made around the same time, which were not disclosed to her.

Bertrand was ultimately laicized (formally removed from the Catholic priesthood) following his conviction for criminal sexual conduct after he pleaded guilty in Minnesota in 2018 to third-degree criminal sexual conduct involving Mastrogiacomo. As part of his sentence, Bertrand received ten years of probation and was required to register as a predatory sex offender. Mastrogiacomo wrote a formal letter of complaint to the late Pope Francis, sent via the Apostolic Nuncio to the United States, Cardinal Christophe Pierre, on September 30, 2024.

In comments directly to me in a May fifth, 2025 telephone conversation, Mastrogiacomo said her letter to Pope Francis "clearly described Cardinal McElroy's complicity in covering up satanic ritual abuse and refusal to work with the criminal prosecutors investigating the felonious crime committed against me by Father Bertrand—which was eventually proven true in a court of law."

"No one may say that Pope Francis was or is ignorant of my criminal case and Cardinal McElroy's criminal complicity. He's not," Mastrogiacomo declared, adding: "In my letter to Pope Francis, I asked, '*How can you and other bishops turn a blind eye to these betrayals?*' I stood up for another woman named Lisa, who pleaded with him as well. I said to the Pope in my letter, "When you refuse to investigate and discipline priests who ritually abuse little girls like Lisa or virgins like me, you send a message that we are not worth protecting. Worst of all, you send a message that our Eucharistic Lord is not worth protecting."

"Three months after I sent the Pope my letter, Pope Francis spat right in my face by promoting Robert McElroy as the Cardinal Archbishop for the Archdiocese of Washington," Mastrogiacomo said. "Far worse than spitting in my face, he spat in the Holy Face of Our Eucharistic Lord." She confronted Cardinal McElroy on March 11, 2025, during his installation Mass as the new archbishop of Washington, DC, at the Basilica of the National Shrine of the Immaculate Conception. Her presence, an embarrassing rebuke to Cardinal McElroy, was intrusively monitored by National Shrine staff, and a stocky woman, identified as Paula Grant, the Secretary for Communications for the Archdiocese of Washington, physically attempted to block Mastrogiacomo from McElroy as he processed into the basilica. At the time she attempted to confront McElroy in the National Shrine, Mastrogiacomo had in her possession, among other sacred items, a small piece of Malachi Martin's corporal cloth he'd used on his altar for saying Mass while still alive.

Rachel Mastrogiacomo's ordeal at the hands of ex-Father Bertrand, compounded by the inaction of and gaslighting by the notoriously heterodox Robert McElroy, until McElroy's hand was forced by pending criminal prosecution of Bertrand, makes it clear the Satanic practices originally documented by Malachi Martin in *Windswept House* were not an isolated aberration or a fictional literary device, but continue at almost every level of the Roman Catholic hierarchy half a century after 1963.

The entire extent of Rachel Mastrogiacomo's ordeal at the hands of Jacob Bertrand, and her subsequent psychological abuse by clerics, all the way up to the late Pope Francis himself, is detailed in her book, *The Devil in Rome: How I Survived Satanic Ritual Abuse by a Catholic Priest*, (Liber Christo Press—2025)

10

THE JESUITS' CHANGING
OF THE GUARD

In a funny way, I became further acquainted with Malachi Martin more thoroughly beyond *Hostage to the Devil* a few years before that dinner on the Upper East Side of Manhattan. After college, I came across his controversial bestseller *The Jesuits*.

What took me aback about *The Jesuits* was that Malachi painstakingly named names, conversations, and a plethora of facts. This nonfiction account of the order revolved around the radical changes in the Jesuits since 1962. *Jesuit* is shorthand for the Society of Jesus religious order founded in 1540 by the youngest son of a noble family from the Basque region of Spain, Iñigo López de Loyola, later known as Saint Ignatius of Loyola. Given that Malachi had spent decades both preparing to be and then as one of the famed "soldiers of the papacy," as the Society of Jesus was known, his book was not based on hearsay or imaginings. Upon reading it, I found it to be a meticulous study of official Jesuit documents, statements, and public actions. Malachi later confided to me that writing it caused not only strong dissension within his own family but cost him a lot of internal pain and soul-searching as well. I remember Malachi telling me that he was able to cope with the nightmares well enough but that reflecting on the facts as presented in the book was hellish, precisely because when he reflected in cold daylight on the facts he presented in the book, it was almost too much to bear.

The Jesuits is a Roman Catholic book; that is to say, it vindicated the prerogatives and status of the pope, whoever he is, and the supernatural, transcendent character of the Church. It also unequivocally delineated the Jesuit ideal, Ignatian spirituality, and the aims of Ignatius of Loyola. It was not a personal document—except that Malachi Martin, a former Jesuit himself, wrote it. As I kept reading, it became clear that only a believing Catholic could write it, and more importantly, only a Jesuit could write it. Only a still-believing Catholic and/or Jesuit would accept the sad facts contained within its pages.

Its direct subject is what the Jesuit order has become since 1965. On this point, it had some heavy criticisms, and names *were* named. This was not deliberate on Malachi's part but was dictated by the source materials. To first understand how corruption entered the Jesuit order, it's necessary to address the elephant in the room: Modernism. Modernism, which had roots stretching back to the French Revolution and beyond, was a religious-philosophical movement that tried to reconcile traditional Church teachings with current advances in science and culture. Ironically enough, one of the standard bearers in the Roman Catholic Church of what Malachi called "that poisonous seed" was a late nineteenth-century Jesuit priest, George Tyrrell, SJ.

Tyrrell was an Irish convert to Roman Catholicism from Anglicanism. He entered the Jesuit order in 1880 and was ordained a priest in 1881. Imbibing the ideas of earlier Modernist clerics and philosophers such as Maurice Blondel and Alfred Loisy, over the next fifteen years, Tyrrell became further enamored with Modernism's central claim that the foundational teachings of Roman Catholicism couldn't be reconciled with modern cultural advances in science, technology, and emerging trends in scriptural scholarship. Modernism taught that God's existence is impervious to reason, and miracles as treated in the New Testament do not prove the foundational claims that the Roman Catholic faith is of divine origin. Perhaps most pernicious of Modernism's tendrils was the line of thought that the structure of the Church and its dogmatic teachings were subject to evolving to keep in step with changing societal and cultural mores.

Although finding great favor among a *sub rosa* group of religious clergy in the late nineteenth century, Pope Pius X recognized Modernism as a lethal poison. The natural outcome of embracing these heretical beliefs was that every foundational belief in the One True Church founded by Jesus Christ was up for grabs because if everything is "true," nothing is true. In a valiant effort to stamp out Modernism, Pope St. Pius X denounced Modernism as "the synthesis of all heresies" and promulgated his encyclical letter to the universal Church entitled *Pascendi Dominici gregis* in 1907, a year after the ex-Father Tyrrell was excommunicated. Despite *Pascendi*, Modernism continued to spread and poison Catholic priests and seminarians alike in *sub rosa* fashion, until it publicly reared its head in the years immediately before and during the Second Vatican Council. Another prominent heretical Jesuit was the infamous Teilhard de Chardin, SJ. Rather than provide an exhaustive treatment of de Chardin's questionable theories on religion, this quote about the heinous medical experiments conducted by the Nazis at the hellish German Dachau concentration camp should suffice that this Jesuit's theology had crossed the line into apostasy, or even a complete departure from the Roman Catholic faith:

> "Once in a debate with Gabriel Marcel on the subject of 'Science and Rationality,' Teilhard shocked his opponent

by refusing to permit even the appalling evidence of the experiments of the Nazi doctors at Dachau to modify his faith in the inevitability of human progress. 'Man,' Teilhard asserted, *'to become full man, **must have tried everything'** ...* (emphasis added). He added that since the human species was still so young...the persistence of such evil was to be expected.[3]

Considering the widespread infection of Modernism among the Jesuits, during dinner one night at the Isle of Capri restaurant, Malachi told me how *The Jesuits* was an incredibly difficult book to write. With a rather rueful look, he spoke of his difficulty criticizing a body of men whom, corporately, he had loved and admired and for whom, as he had once known them, he would be forever lonely and exiled from. He loved the old Society before its infection with Modernism and the old Society that was being laid viciously and gleefully to rest. A new *thing*—anti-papal, un-Catholic, pagan in its tendencies, much like the monster in Mary Shelley's Frankenstein— was being built and substituted for the old Society of Jesus, and enforced silence, brazen tolerance, enshrouded all.

Malachi still had very good friends in the Society, in Rome, in the U.S., and elsewhere. He told me that the time for the book was now, and not later. In the Roman Church of the 1980s, there was a battle going on that endures to the current day—a battle for the Roman Catholic Church, of which he was a priest, and a battle for the Petrine privilege. No book has handled the core subject: why and how the Society of Jesus has corporately become the clever enemy of the papacy and of Roman Catholic teaching, as vindicated by the Church Councils and the popes of Rome.

---

1.   Mary Lukas and Ellen Lukas, *Teilhard* (Garden City, New York: Doubleday, 1977): 237-8.

I told Malachi that I was planning on re-reading the book considering our new friendship. I asked him if the book would confuse Catholics, given the laity's long-standing respect for the Jesuits. He responded, "Rob, when you read it, you will find that, no, far from confusing, it draws very clear lines, explains what is confusing, and reiterates traditional Catholic doctrine. It can only clarify. And encourage. And confirm. And enlighten. If only a percentage of Catholics in the United States had protested in time, you wouldn't now have the shambles you see all around you. Don't you see the progressively more extensive rot every day? And shouldn't you start screaming? Aren't you allowing confusion to get more confounded? Will your passing from the human scene, silent, have aided or disabled the Church?" I will remember these as some of the most accusatorily stark words ever uttered by my best friend. I felt like crawling under a rock.

When I continued to press the issue in a subsequent letter, that wasn't he kicking the hornet's nest, he gave me an answer I will never forget: "Will there be trouble? Yes, for *me*. The Jesuits involved will throw every bit of mud and dirt they can pick up from the terrain I have traveled since 1964 and then some of their own arbitrary choosing. *Jusuita Jesuitae lupissimus!* (Jesuit Jesuits most wolfish!) Do I fear it? Yes, I fear it. I fear all hate and humiliation. So did Christ. Should I not have published it on that account? Come on, Rob, you should know better.

"You ask me what honest priests would say about the accusations and revelations in the book? I think what they would say is as follows:

"We and our generation of priests, bishops, theologians, and intellectual leaders have failed. When there was a definite destruction of the Catholic Church going on under our eyes, we went along with it. Why? *There was nothing in our seminary training about what a priest was to do when officialdom introduced heresy and schism and clever derogations of Marian devotion and subtle sacrilege.* For example, nobody ever told us what to do when senior clergy were revealed to be Masons. And worst of all, no one trained us to recognize a loss of faith in our fellow clerics. Bishops and priests just didn't lose faith. Besides, we didn't want to rock the boat. You simply didn't go against the consensus at your priests' conference; you didn't tell the bishop he was either a material heretic or an ignoramus, a knave or a fool. We were trained not to rock the boat. Now the Modernists have destroyed structures of faith and morality, which took hundreds of years and generations of sweat and saints to build up.

"My point is: we have gone far enough. Too far. If we do not protest, what are the ordinary laity like yourself to think? Of course, I'm going to die. We're all going to die someday. But 'you must live and act as if you were not going to die, and you must pray and do good works as if your last moment has come' (Saint Augustine). I will not do something or abstain from doing what I should do merely because I am over seventy. Leave all that heavy stuff to the Lord of life and death.

"More precisely, because I am going to die and am on the home stretch, I have to do my 'bit,' do what I see should be done, act as if it all depended on me while praying and realizing that it all depends on God. Will it do good? I am convinced it will undo evil and do good. So, say all my advisors, Jesuit and non-Jesuit. It will enhance the Church's image and the Holy Father's image. I cannot see myself facing Jesus at my judgment and saying: 'No, I didn't speak out, Lord. I thought it was too close to my death.' The Lord Jesus could well retort: 'And I, *What about me? Wasn't I near my death?* And didn't I give you the brains, the experience, and the chance to tell it like it was? *Tell me, Malachi, **do you deserve to come home right now?**'*

"Now for a few moments, think back what once, twenty years ago, was the devotion to the Sacred Heart—nine Fridays, the five First Saturdays as requested by Our Lady of Fatima, consecration, reparation, devotion to the Blessed Sacrament, daily Holy Communion, weekly confession, religion properly taught to school children, confraternities, sodalities, Benediction of the Blessed Sacrament, the network of religious societies, the Rosary, the devotion to the Holy Souls in Purgatory, devotion to the Holy Father and absolute moral rules against fornication, cohabitation, homosexuality, lesbianism, abortion, contraception and reception of the Blessed Sacrament by civilly divorced and remarried Catholics. Think about all that has been destroyed in mere years! And about the Jesuits who have deserted the defense of the Pontiff and their duty to defend Catholicism. Instead, they have gleefully participated in its destruction.

"The godless and the servants of Lucifer want us silent and dead so that the demolition of the Church can continue and the assimilation of Catholicism to the middle-class values of a secular, godless society can continue unhindered. We are fighting against what is now recognized as the *de facto* abolition of Christianity in our Western culture. It's violent. It's to the death."

It has become even more starkly clear that despite Malachi's vigorous personal opposition, Modernism was widely adopted by the Jesuit order in the late 1950s and 1960s due to its rather neat alignment with the Marxist teachings of Sardinian Communist Antonio Gramsci, who advocated the subversion of Catholic dogma by emptying it of divine, transcendent theology. The Jesuits, historically a powerful force active in fighting evil, became turncoats against the papacy, betraying the ideals of their founder, *Ignacio de Loyola* or Ignatius of Loyola, and Malachi couldn't accept this act of betrayal. Since *The Jesuits* was published, we have witnessed an about-face by the once stalwart order devoted to the papacy and Catholic tradition. In the last several decades, Jesuits have run the heterodox gamut from being enthusiastic participants in the Nicaraguan government's Sandinista Marxist dictatorship (Father Fernando Cardenal, SJ, and Father Miguel D'Escoto, SJ, both became senior officials in the new Marxist Nicaraguan government, and the ex-Jesuit Father James Carney took up arms against the Honduran government) to now having Jesuit Father James Martin, SJ, an ultra-prominent homosexual rights activist, serving at the late Jesuit Pope Francis's request on the Vatican Dicastery for Communications since 2017.

I can only imagine my late friend would weep for what Iñigo López de Loyola's band of brothers has become.

The author and Malachi Martin in Livanos apt, 1994.

The author and Malachi Martin in Livanos family apt, 1996.

Our Lady of Mt. Carmel.

Malachi fencing.

Robert Marro Jr.

Malachi Martin in Cairo circa 1951.

The author meeting Pope John Paul II, 1995.

Malachi Martin

Malachi Martin.

Malachi Martin (second from left) Aviano AFB circa 1957.

Malachi Martin playing at a ruined castle.

Malachi Martin in Rome.

Malachi Martin with his father, Doctor Conor
Martin, and his brothers circa 1926.

Malachi age six and sister Netta age
four. Photo studio circa 1927.

Malachi Martin with his family at the beach circa 1927.

Taken in Skerries / Dad and ourselves with Gabbo Moloney and his sister. Mauleus is Not in it. — Sadey Mauleus is in photo Not Gabbos' sister

BACK ROW: Bill, Daddy, me
middle row: Connie, Frank, a friend,
front row: Moura, Kitty holding Kay, Joan

Back of photo.

Malachi Martin's father, Doctor Conor Martin.

Malachi Martin defending his doctoral thesis.

1 1

MASS CONFUSION

Malachi Martin had a unique window into the inner workings of the Vatican, and this was not limited to close conversations with various popes and cardinals but the very fabric of daily life within Vatican City State itself. One subject Malachi had *very* strong opinions on was that of the Roman Catholic Mass itself, especially regarding the changes made in the wake of the Second Vatican Council. The Mass, or the Holy Sacrifice of the Mass as it is properly called when said by a validly ordained priest, is held by Catholics to be a bloodless re-presentation of the supreme sacrifice made by the Lord Jesus when the Son of God was crucified at Golgotha outside the walls of Jerusalem some two thousand years ago. For continuity, when I refer to the "Traditional Latin Mass," I'm referring to the pre-1962 Mass. I will refer to the new Mass of Pope Paul VI by its common Latin moniker of the *"Novus Ordo Missae"* or simply the "New Mass." In starting this chapter, **I want to stress that I am not an expert on the theological intricacies of the pre-1962 Traditional Roman Mass or the 1969 New Mass of Paul VI.** I am only repeating what Malachi Martin told me; he was most emphatic on the following.

Most American Catholics today are only familiar with the English-language vernacular *Novus Ordo Missae,* or the "New Mass."

It was promulgated in 1969 by Pope Paul VI after several years of development by the *Consilium* organization, headed by Monsignor Annibale Bugnini, to this day a lightning rod for conservative and traditionalist critics. In addition to Roman clerics and liturgical experts, the *Consilium* also included the assistance of six Protestant observers. These were:

1. Max Thurian (Calvinist–Ecumenical Community of Taize)
2. Friedrich Künneth (Lutheran)
3. Raymond George (Methodist)
4. Ronald Jaspar (Anglican)
5. Eugene Brand (Lutheran)
6. Massey Shepherd (Episcopalian)

Malachi Martin accepted the validity of the New Mass; however, he repeatedly told me that the New Mass produced by the *Consilium* and its Protestant advisors was sorely deficient compared to the Traditional Latin Mass. He hammered home that unless a priest was *very* conscientious regarding the prayers and gestures used in the New Mass, especially in the English vernacular, there was a likelihood such Masses were invalid. Invalid in the sense that the priest did not affect the miracle of transubstantiation, where the unleavened bread and wine truly became the Body, Blood, Soul, and Divinity of the Lord Jesus.

Malachi told me that, in contrast to those Roman Catholics who insist that there are *three* essential conditions for a valid Catholic Mass to occur, there are *four* necessary conditions. The traditional elements needed for a valid Roman Mass are the following: valid *matter*, in other words, proper unleavened bread and grape wine, as neither hot dog buns, raisin nut bread, or grape-flavored Kool-Aid would be liturgically appropriate bread and wine for use during Mass. Next would be the proper *form* of the prayers that transubstantiate the bread and wine into the Body and Blood of Christ. The essential elements of these prayers, taking as an example the Roman Canon (and post-Vatican II Eucharistic Prayer Number One, which is *modeled after* the traditional Roman Canon from the Traditional Latin Mass but is *not* identical to it), are *"HOC EST ENIM CORPUS MEUM"* (FOR THIS IS MY BODY) and *"HIC EST ENIM CALIX SANGUINIS MEI, NOVI ET AETERNI TESTAMENTI: MYSTERIUM FIDEI: QUI PRO VOBIS ET PRO MULTIS EFFUNDETUR IN REMISSIONEM PECCATORUM"* (FOR THIS IS THE CHALICE OF MY BLOOD, OF THE NEW AND ETERNAL TESTAMENT: THE MYSTERY OF FAITH: WHICH SHALL BE SHED FOR YOU AND FOR MANY UNTO THE REMISSION OF SINS). Lastly, the priest must intend to do what the Church intends in confecting the Blessed Sacrament and Precious Blood.

Most Catholic theologians and qualified liturgists stop at these three. Still, Malachi told me that a critical *fourth element* must be present after Vatican II's changes. That element is that the priest offering the Holy Sacrifice of the Mass must be *validly ordained* to do what the Church intends at Mass. When I asked him why Catholics can be permitted to doubt the validity of what I will refer to here as post-1968 *Novus Ordo*-era ordinations, he replied that changes to the actual rite of ordination for priests rendered them dubiously effective. When I pressed him on this topic, Malachi said that in the traditional pre-1968 rite of priestly ordination found in the *Roman Pontifical*, the official Roman Catholic book used for ordaining deacons, priests, and bishops, the ordaining bishop performed three critical actions that left no doubt about the validity of priestly ordination. First, the hands of the *ordinand* (prospective priest) were specifically anointed and consecrated. Second, the new priest was presented with a paten (to hold the host during Mass) and chalice (to hold the wine during Mass), and specifically told by the bishop, "*Receive the power to offer sacrifice to God, and to celebrate Masses for the living as well as for the dead, in the name of the Lord.*" However, Pope Paul VI authorized changes that did not specifically state this conferral of power, as the new rite of ordination only says, "*Accept from the holy people of God the gifts to be offered to him.*" Finally, the traditional ordination concludes with the bishop conferring a final "power" to the new priest: "*Receive the Holy Ghost, whose sins thou shalt forgive, they are forgiven them; and whose sins thou shalt retain, they are retained.*" This part of the sacrament of Holy Orders was *completely omitted* under Pope Paul VI.[4]

Being a theological neophyte of the highest order, I somewhat flippantly asked Malachi why this was a cause for controversy, as I was a layman who had always believed the maxim "The pope said this is now the way it is, so shut up and obey." He patiently told me that given the extreme state of flux in Roman Catholic seminary formation for Catholic priests since 1968, traditional Catholic academic teaching emphasis on the writings of such Roman Catholic

1. For the reference of any interested reader, I have taken the preceding words of ordination for priests ordained in the older pre-Vatican II rite from the 1924

   RITE OF ORDINATION ACCORDING TO THE ROMAN PONTIFICAL BY THE Right Rev. J. S. M. LYNCH, LL.D., D.D.
   Fourth Edition, Revised and Enlarged.
   Published by The Cathedral Library Association © 1924, 24-26 East 21st Street, New York, New York.

   For the new post-Vatican II 1968 ordination of a priest, who was now officially referred to as a *presbyter*, I have used the wording as found in the

   ROMAN PONTIFICAL REVISED BY DECREE OF THE SECOND VATICAN ECUMENICAL COUNCIL AND PUBLISHED BY AUTHORITY OF POPE PAUL VI
   PUBLISHED BY THE INTERNATIONAL COMMISSION ON ENGLISH IN THE LITURGY © 1978

luminaries as St. Thomas Aquinas, St. Alphonsus Liguori, and St. Robert Bellarmine was largely scrapped or greatly de-emphasized. In the place of their scholasticism, a "new theology," or "*Nouvelle théologie*" as its proponents called it, nourished by the Modernist ideas of heterodox theologians such as Karl Rahner, SJ, Hans Küng, Edward Schillebeeckx, OP, Yves Congar, and Henri de Lubac came into vogue. These heretical theologians claimed that their *Nouvelle théologie* was in many ways a return to the teachings of the original early Church fathers, but they were rebutted by such eminent ortho-dox theologians as Réginald Garrigou-Lagrange, OP, who averred their "new theology" was merely the Modernism condemned by Pope St. Pius X under a different name.

An example of heresy introduced into the Eucharistic Prayers (and then belatedly corrected in 1985 when pointed out, but *not* before official promulgation for several years) can be found in the original English-language preface prayer for Eucharistic Prayer Number Four. As promulgated in English, the preface prayer orig-inally read:

> *Father in Heaven*
> *It is right that we should give you thanks and glory.*
> ***You alone are God***, *living and true...* (emphasis mine)

Malachi said that when taken at face value, the phrase "you alone are God" was a denial of the sacred doctrine of the Holy Trinity and the divinity of Jesus. It was a prayer that the ancient heretic Arius would be perfectly happy with, as his heresy of Arianism also denied the divinity of Jesus.

"What does this have to do with the New Mass?" I asked Malachi. He told me that based on two letters allegedly found in his briefcase, the architect of the New Mass, Annibale Bugnini, was the subject of much speculation that he was a Freemason codenamed "Buan" charged by the Masonic lodge in Italy with adulterating, watering down, and corrupting the traditional Roman Mass. Malachi did not hold a very high opinion of Monsignor (later Archbishop) Bugnini. He told me that evidence of Bugnini's treachery was presented to a bewildered and then, by turn, angry Pope Paul VI in 1975, but not in the manner that most traditionalist Roman Catholic pundits would have it. Malachi vehemently insisted on more than one occasion that not only was Bugnini a Freemason, but when a delegation of senior Roman clergy brought the proof of Bugnini's membership in Freemasonry to Pope Paul VI, they had an unexpected ace up their sleeve. They also brought several black and white photographs taken in the early 1950s of Pope Paul VI himself, as Monsignor Giovanni Battista Montini, being initiated into Freemasonry. Malachi did not show me such photos; however, I have no reason to doubt him. What is indisputable is that shortly after this alleged evidence was provided of Pope Paul VI, Annibale Bugnini was appointed the papal *nuncio*, or papal ambassador to Iran. In the mid-1970s, Iran under the Shah and later the ayatollahs was a Catholic backwater akin to being symbolically exiled to an ecclesial Siberia.

Malachi Martin never celebrated the New Mass, only the Traditional Latin Mass.

As a postscript to Malachi's warnings about the validity of the New Mass, it was revealed in a May 2023 letter from Archbishop Joseph Naumann, archbishop of Kansas City, Kansas, that priests had approached him from different parishes in his archdiocese who had discovered an objectively scandalous situation. They determined that the wine used at the New Mass was not valid matter to confect the precious Blood of Jesus. This was due to the inclusion in the alleged sacramental wine of adulterating ingredients, such as elderberry extract, sugars, and additional alcohol, which made the wine invalid for use at Mass. This had been taking place at various parishes throughout his archdiocese for years since Vatican II and was of such grave importance that Archbishop Naumann had to petition the Vatican for a remedy. **The potentially tens or hundreds of thousands of invalid Masses** in the Archdiocese of Kansas City, Kansas, whether for Sunday Mass, weddings, funerals, Gregorian Masses offered for the repose of the dead...or any other celebrated Mass, were now potentially nothing more than Protestant memorial services where the congregation sees the liturgy as a mere "memorial of the Lord," and Jesus is not truly made present. This results in many cases from parish "liturgy committees" being responsible for procuring supplies for Mass, and in their quest for frugality, they purchase cases of "Two Buck Chuck" from a Trader Joe's grocery store. Never mind that it wasn't valid sacramental wine, *it was on sale.*

To engage in an extrapolation of the grave nature of this situation, according to the USCCB (United States Conference of Catholic Bishops), there are about 16,700 parishes in the United States. Most of these parishes have similar liturgy committees responsible for buying wine for Mass. For illustration purposes, let's say that one-tenth or 1,670 parishes inadvertently used invalid wine at Mass. If each parish had eleven Masses per week, fifty-two weeks a year, that comes to 955,240 invalid Masses (including the aforementioned weddings, funerals...and more) per year. Let's extend this to beginning in the heady days after Vatican II, where experimentation with Mass was the name of the game. Picking 1975 as the start date would mean at least forty-eight years of invalid Masses nationwide, or *almost forty-six million invalid Masses in the United States alone.* According to the internationally known and respected priest and blogger Father John Zuhlsdorf, in a post at his wdtprs.com website on June 5, 2023, when he learned of the situation in Kansas City, he wrote, *"There is hardly anything crueler that a priest can do than to leave people in doubt about the validity of their sacraments. It is extremely VEXING to learn of priests who are so thick...so arrogant...that they can't or won't be exacting about the VALIDITY of sacraments. It isn't hard. You* '**Say The Black and Do The Red**,' *and you use valid matter.*"

Finally, to rhetorically repeat Malachi's question, "Is the New Mass in the vernacular always valid?" we turn to the confusingly named 2022-2024 Vatican "Synod on Synodality." As of November 15, 2024, the Vatican's Dicastery for Divine Worship and the Discipline of the Sacraments has "with the authority of the Pope, on November 8 of this year, granted the long-awaited recognition of some liturgical adaptations for the celebration of the Holy Mass in the Tseltal, Tsotsil, Ch'ol, Tojolabal, and Zoque ethnic groups of the diocese of San Cristóbal de Las Casas." This is a "development" of the *Novus Ordo* of Pope Paul VI to meld the service with local traditions and customs, elements of which are problematic from the traditional Roman Catholic perspective. Some aspects of the so-called new "Mayan Mass" are arguably pagan and incompatible with Roman Catholicism.

But this is not the end of the "adaptation" of the Mass of Paul VI. Malachi told me more than once efforts were already underway within progressive, Modernist Vatican factions, again in cooperation with representatives of Protestant denominations, to further "develop" the *Novus Ordo Missae* of Paul VI. The aim is to promulgate an ecumenical liturgical service at which all Reformation and post-Reformation Christian Protestant denominations, such as Anglicans, Lutherans, Presbyterians, Baptists, Pentecostals, United Church of Christ...and more, could comfortably worship alongside Roman Catholics without conceding their heretical beliefs incompatible with Roman Catholicism. This ecumenical "Mass" has been provisionally dubbed the *Ritus Simplex* or "Simple Rite."

Malachi said to avoid offending evangelical Protestant sensibilities, it would almost certainly exclude the traditional Catholic words of Consecration, which the Catholic priest uses to effect transubstantiation and call down Christ upon the altar, thus resulting in an invalid "Mass." Malachi believed the *Ritus Simplex* would be the fulfillment of the prophecy of the Hebrew prophet Daniel, who stated in Chapter 12:11, *"And from the time **when the continual sacrifice shall be taken away**, and the abomination of desolation shall be set up..."* Malachi believed formal Vatican promulgation of the *Ritus Simplex* would be the "abomination of desolation" spoken of by Daniel and that this was also referenced in the unrevealed Third Secret of Fatima.

We have been warned.

1 2

COMMUTING A DEATH SENTENCE

In 1994, while living in New York City, I befriended a young woman who worked out at the New York Sports Club near my apartment. Her name was Laura F. She was an actress on a CBS soap opera. Although she was from the Reform tradition of Judaism, it didn't stop us from forming a fast friendship at the time. Although true to her faith, she became fascinated with my description of Malachi Martin and the topic of exorcism. She'd never met a Catholic priest before, so she eagerly accepted the invitation when I asked if she'd like to accompany me to one of my informal lunches with Malachi at the "greasy spoon diner" on Lexington Avenue. Malachi was delighted to meet her and answer her wide-eyed questions. He easily answered her questions about possession and exorcism with his trademark Irish charm, which she did not know outside of television and movie depictions. She subsequently became an occasional guest at our lunches, and Malachi was always delighted to see her accompany me.

One day in mid-1996, while working out at the gym, I noticed Laura was distracted and subdued. I started a conversation with her and soon realized something was bothering her. We met for lunch the next day near Lincoln Center, and she was distracted and near tears. As a case officer for the Agency, I had been thoroughly trained in elicitation techniques, including getting people to open up about their problems. I gently told her, "You know, you might feel a little better if you talk about whatever is on your mind." She told me that her sister-in-law Jessica, who had just delivered a healthy baby boy via C-section, was at Mount Sinai Hospital and was suffering from late-stage acute myeloid leukemia (AML), an aggressive, relatively uncommon cancer that affects the patient's bone marrow and blood. When I asked if Jessica was responding to her chemotherapy, Laura completely broke down in the restaurant. She said that the doctors told her sister-in-law that if Laura went through with beginning chemotherapy treatment, there was a very high likelihood Jessica would have a miscarriage and lose her unborn child.

After a lot of emotional back-and-forth, Jessica decided to hold off on starting chemotherapy until her unborn child was old enough to be safely delivered by C-section. The doctors in the Mount Sinai oncology department strongly advised against Jessica following this course of action, as delaying her leukemia treatment until her child was born could be fatal. Laura told me Jessica was adamant about not starting chemotherapy until her baby was safely delivered. Laura was already showing some of the classic symptoms of AML, such as easy bruising, fatigue, unexplained nosebleeds, persistent infections, and weight loss for no apparent reason. The diagnosis was confirmed when Jessica began having regular blood tests, which revealed the typical extreme deviations in white blood cell count from the normal average.

Fast-forward six weeks, and Jessica delivered a very healthy baby boy, albeit just over a month premature. One heartbreaking aspect of having given birth to her son while she was suffering from AML was that Jessica couldn't hold her child after he was born. This was because her healthy baby, now in the hospital nursery, carried normal germs that were normally of no consequence but could kill a mother suffering from AML because his mother had a suppressed immune system that couldn't fight off the most inconsequential infection. Jessica promptly began regular rounds of chemotherapy; however, because she had delayed treatment for the sake of her son, the leukemia proceeded to ravage her system. In short order, Jessica rapidly lost her hair and almost thirty-five pounds. That very morning before Laura and I met for lunch, Jessica's doctors, who had terrible bedside manners, told Jessica's husband that he needed to accept the reality of his wife's situation and prepare for her death. The entire family was understandably devastated.

Later that afternoon, I called Laura and asked if Jessica's husband or family would be offended if I asked if Malachi would be willing to visit Jessica and give her a blessing. Even though the family was Jewish, I asked this in the spirit of "any port in a storm." I was surprised when the family said they would welcome a visit to Jessica from Malachi, whom they heard of from Laura. It was a sign of the doctors' pessimism regarding Jessica's prognosis that they consented to people visiting Jessica at all, given her severe degree of immunosuppression and accompanying risk of infection. I called up Malachi and explained Jessica's dire medical prognosis. I asked him if he would accompany me to Mount Sinai and give Laura's sister-in-law Jessica a blessing. Malachi readily agreed, and we arranged to visit Mount Sinai Hospital the next morning.

Malachi and I entered Jessica's hospital room the next day, where her husband, Michael, and Laura were waiting. As was his custom, Malachi wore a cream-colored Irish cable knit sweater, dark blue sports jacket, and matching slacks. Jessica looked up from her sunken eyes at Malachi with the sad desperation of someone given a death sentence and yet still hoping beyond hope it wasn't true. Malachi asked Jessica and her husband, Michael, if they would mind if he imparted a special blessing. Malachi then took out a small container holding chrism oil made from specially blessed olive oil and balsam, an aromatic additive. He pressed his thumb against the cotton pad holding the chrism oil and proceeded to anoint Jessica's forehead with the Sign of the Cross while softly reciting a prayer in Latin. He then removed a small reliquary from his blazer's inner pocket, and after making the Sign of the Cross over her, he touched the small reliquary to Jessica's forehead, softly whispering another blessing in Latin.

At the end of the short *ad hoc* ceremony, Jessica looked sadly up at Malachi and plaintively asked him, "Am I going to die?" Malachi looked back and emphatically answered, "No, ma'am. You're **not** going to die." We then bid them goodbye and proceeded to the elevator to take us back to the lobby. While we were in the elevator, Malachi became angry with me for the only time I knew him. I asked Malachi, "When Jessica asked you if she was going to die, and you told her she wouldn't, were you saying that the same way people try to cheer up someone with a terminal disease diagnosis by telling them to stay positive because doctors are always researching new medicines and treatment?"

Malachi rounded on me as the elevator descended and fixed me with a stare that would've frozen boiling water. Although he didn't say a word, it wasn't necessary. The look on his face reprimanded me with a silent, "Oh ye of little faith." In my defense, I was hoping Malachi's visit would cheer Jessica and her family up, if only for a little while. We rode in silence back to his apartment, where I dropped him off. It wasn't until late the next morning that I received an excited call from Laura, who was giddy with joy.

"What's going on?" I asked. Laura's voice practically exploded out of the phone receiver.

"It's NORMAL!!!" she cried exuberantly. *"It's **ALL** NORMAL...!"* Distracted by the small mountain of paperwork on my desk, I didn't immediately realize what Laura was referring to until she said, "Jessica had her blood tested last night and again this morning, and the results came back completely *normal* for her white blood cell count!" It took me a moment to process what she was saying, and I croaked out incredulously, "Are you *sure*...?"

Laura explained that Jessica had her first blood test in the early evening following Malachi's visit and that her white cell count had inexplicably reverted to near-normal levels. Fearing some mistake in their testing methodology, especially where a grave disease like AML was concerned, they ran a complete panel of blood tests again the next morning. This time, the tests displayed a normal white blood cell count for a thirty-year-old woman. More importantly, additional tests revealed no trace of the deadly cancer that had ravaged her frail body only a day before. The oncology doctors at Mount Sinai were at a complete loss to explain the sudden disappearance of leukemia, and they went so far as to admit to Jessica and her overjoyed family they had no rational scientific explanation for why Jessica was now cancer-free. Being doctors (and rationalist skeptics as well), they would not say Jessica's cure was a *miracle*, but despite their collective expertise, they could find no way to explain it. AML was a disease you didn't just wake up and find yourself spontaneously healed from.

Immediately after this episode, Malachi had to be out of town for several days, and I could not contact him. When we met the next week, I couldn't wait to tell him the good news. I thanked him for blessing Jessica and healing her. Malachi quickly responded, "*I* didn't heal her, Rob," with an emphasis on "I." I asked him what saint's relic he blessed Jessica with, and Malachi replied quietly.

"It was a splinter of the True Cross...."

To this day, I still shake my head in wonder. Was it a miracle? The doctors at Mount Sinai wouldn't say no.

1 3

THE INCIDENT AT FORT BRAGG

One of the more bizarre events that occurred during the years I was privileged to know Malachi came in 1991, and it involved possession and exorcism, but not in the usual way people who've taken a more than cursory look into the topic might think. Most people with more than a passing knowledge of Malachi know his best-selling 1976 book *Hostage to the Devil.* It was, as the cover described at the time of publication, the true story of the possession and exorcism of five living Americans. Most of these people have passed away in the forty-four years since its publication, but the book gave a far more nuanced view into a phenomenon that first exploded into America's popular consciousness with the 1973 motion picture starring Linda Blair, *The Exorcist.* The movie, which became a runaway hit and pop culture phenomenon, was modern America's first real introduction to an arcane topic previously kept deep under wraps by the Roman Catholic Church. The modern Church in the United States, still adjusting to the seismic changes introduced by the Second Vatican Council, wasn't keen on Americans' newfound fascination with a subject that was seen by many clergy as an embarrassing medieval relic. The concept of Personal Evil didn't fit very well with an American church that increasingly looked at evil with a small *e*, where it was seen in terms of societal problems, such as racism and poverty, not to mention the ongoing Vietnam War.

Just when the American Church had jettisoned the Traditional Latin Mass, nuns were wearing fashionable outfits, and rosary beads were more likely to be adorning car rear-view mirrors than passing through Catholic fingers, *The Exorcist* flashed in lurid R-rated gore that scared the wits out of the moviegoing public. Rectories across the United States were besieged with calls from Catholics and non-Catholics alike who were convinced the Devil possessed them. Malachi released his book *Hostage to the Devil* three years later, in 1976, which soon rocketed up the bestseller charts. In subsequent radio and television appearances to promote the book, Malachi made no bones about his opinion of *The Exorcist*, calling it a "typical Hollywood Frankenstein-Dracula horror movie, with spinning heads and lots of green goop." Malachi went to great pains to debunk the myths surrounding *The Exorcist*, adamant in his view that demonic possession was much more lethal than portrayed in the movie because, in reality, it dealt with the struggle of human wills helplessly in thrall to the Prince of Darkness and his minions.

With one notable exception, Malachi, who often served as an assistant priest in many exorcisms, never involved me as an assistant in the actual rite itself. Perhaps it was due to my career as a CIA officer, or maybe he had an insight into my personality that told him I'd be unsuited for the task; I'll never know. We did develop a tag-team approach when he was involved in exorcisms. When he was involved in an exorcism, I would frequently go to a local church and pray the Rosary in front of Jesus in the Blessed Sacrament, asking for the intercession of the Lord and His Mother for the safety of all involved in the hideous affair. Malachi told me that, in his experience, it came in two varieties, both of which took a toll on the exorcist. The first types were those exorcisms that involved a confrontation with the Evil Spirit on an intellectual level, where the evil entity hid behind the victim's personality, and the exorcist had to wear down this "Pretense" as Malachi called it. The second type of exorcism was what Malachi called a "dirty exorcism," where the possessed demonstrated preternatural phenomena inexplicable to modern science. These were the confrontations with Personal Evil with an element of the macabre and grotesque, most often involving the afflicted person vomiting copious amounts of materials such as glass shards, nails, living worms...and so forth that would fill a typical orange Home Depot bucket. It was a demonstration of power by the Evil Spirit that it was capable of inflicting trauma not just on the possessed but all involved in the exorcism.

This often happened after Malachi breached the "Pretense" stage of the exorcism, where the demon was forced to stop hiding behind the victim's personality. This stage, which Malachi called the "Breakpoint," inevitably led to the "Clash." This was the direct confrontation between the possessing demon and the exorcist acting *in personae Christi*, or in the person of Christ. The Clash often took a physical toll on the exorcist, and I witnessed this many times in Malachi. I'd call him, and there was an ineffable weariness in his voice, as if his very soul had suffered an indescribable trauma.

All of this served as the backdrop to the strangest instance of demonic possession and subsequent exorcism I ever experienced with Malachi. I remember Malachi called me one day in 1991 after Operation Desert Storm and asked if I'd accompany him on a one-day trip to the Pentagon in Northern Virginia via the Amtrak Metroliner. Later that day, when we met for lunch, Malachi elaborated that he'd been contacted by a high-ranking Catholic aide to SECDEF (Secretary of Defense) Dick Cheney, who asked if Malachi would agree to come to Washington in a few weeks to give his opinion on a particularly vexing problem. I eagerly agreed to be Malachi's traveling companion and put in for a vacation day. The following week, I picked Malachi up at his apartment on East 63rd Street very early one morning to catch the first Metroliner to DC. The trip to Amtrak Union Station in Washington took almost three hours, and we probably talked about every topic under the sun there and back. As an aside, I wondered afterward in a detached sort of way, *I just got to spend six hours on a train with Malachi Martin*, in the same mundane way someone might say, "I just spent six hours painting the garage…" From my current vantage point, some thirty-four years later, I look back on how incredibly blessed I was that God's plan brought this holy Renaissance man of a priest into my life on a day-to-day basis.

After arriving in Washington, we took the Metro subway system to the Pentagon stop. **I want to stress that I was there as Malachi's private citizen traveling companion and *not in any capacity* as a representative of my employer at the time, the CIA.** I want to set this part of the record straight, as people will draw unwarranted inferences that the Agency was somehow involved due to my presence when this couldn't be further from the truth. I was merely present as Rob, Malachi's Catholic friend from New York City. At the time, Malachi was almost seventy, and, when possible, he greatly preferred to have a good friend along when he had to travel for private matters that did not involve the promotion of his books.

We alighted at the Metro Pentagon stop, where we made our way to the entrance and were greeted by an army officer. He led us on a confusing, circuitous trek through the concentric pentagonal buildings that make up the Pentagon until we arrived at an ordinary conference room. Upon entering, we were greeted by approximately eight people, split evenly between what I assume were Department of Defense civilian executives and uniformed military officers seated at a large conference table. I was told to sit at one of the chairs along the wall while Malachi was seated at the conference table with the "important people." It felt like one of those Thanksgiving dinners where the grownups sit at the main table, and the kids are put off to the side, but I didn't care. Malachi was greeted by the aide to SECDEF Cheney, whom we'll call Thomas. Thomas performed the introductions around the room. I don't recall any of the names, but I do remember that there was a one-star brigadier general, a colonel, a lieutenant colonel, and a couple of lower-ranking army officers. Besides the aide to SECDEF, I don't remember any of the civilians who were in attendance, except that there were a psychiatrist and psychologist.

After the Pentagon representatives were introduced, Malachi was introduced as "Dr. Martin from New York," and there was no mention that he was either a Roman Catholic priest or an exorcist. He wore a high-collar gray sweater, blue slacks, and a navy blazer. Thomas then got right to the point, saying that a military unit at Fort Bragg, North Carolina, had been engaged in "unorthodox psychological training methods" that aimed to use untapped powers of the human mind to gain a military advantage over America's adversaries in war. I was seated against the wall opposite Malachi and, when this statement was made, saw his eyes narrow for the briefest moment; otherwise, he gave no discernable reaction.

Then, one of the military officers picked up a phone. A few moments later, a young female officer introduced as "Carol," wearing Desert Storm–style BDU (Battle Dress Uniform) fatigues, entered escorted by three burly military policemen. She looked to be maybe five foot four and weighed about 120 pounds. There was nothing distinctive or remarkable about her, and Malachi gave no reaction when she entered. Then, one of the DoD shrinks addressed

"Carol" and said she would perform some training demonstrations to demonstrate her progress in "the program."

She was then instructed to demonstrate "extreme weight." "Carol" then closed her eyes as the psychiatrist or psychologist counted backward from ten. She opened her eyes, and the MPs who escorted her into the room tried to lift her. From the effort and grunting noises they were making, it seemed like they were trying to lift a cement truck. "Carol" was then instructed to "end the exercise," and she closed her eyes as the doctor counted backward from ten again. When she opened her eyes, just one of the MPs could lift her easily.

The next instruction was for Carol to demonstrate "immovability." Again, the same procedure was followed, wherein Carol closed her eyes as the psychiatrist/psychologist counted down from ten. She then opened her eyes with a neutral look on her face. The doctor running the demonstration nodded to the MPs who suddenly rushed at Carol with the clear intent of tackling her. When they bounced off her like they were trying to tackle a telephone pole, I felt a pit in my stomach; something was wrong here. Again, I glanced at Malachi, and his face displayed no reaction. At the end of this exercise, two MPs grabbed each of Carol's arms and could easily tug her back and forth like they were playing tug of war.

Finally, the most disturbing demonstration of Carol's mental warfare abilities came. A piece of heavy wood like an oaken kitchen butcher block was removed from where it leaned against the wall and placed on the conference room table. I recall that it was approximately eighteen inches square and two inches thick. Carol was instructed to demonstrate "digital penetration without physical injury." Carol had delicate hands with neatly trimmed nails, done in a short French-manicure style. With her palm facing down on the butcher block, she lifted her hand so only her fingertips were touching the butcher block. Again, the same protocol was followed, wherein she closed her eyes; however, her eyes remained closed when the doctor finished counting down from ten. Throughout the next two to three minutes, her fingertips gradually began to penetrate the butcher block. Although Malachi gave no reaction, I, on the other hand, felt a nauseating fear wash over me as I did my level best to remain in control of my bladder. There was a palpable air of *wrongness* as Carol finally opened her eyes and pulled her hand away from the butcher block without visible damage to her fingernails or hand. But impressed there on the surface of the butcher block, to a depth of perhaps half an inch, were clear impressions in the hardwood where her fingers made contact.

Then, Carol was escorted from the room by the hulking MPs. Malachi remarked in a neutral tone that her demonstrations were remarkable as he lightly touched the butcher block where the impressions of her fingertips remained. He then looked at Thomas and asked why he had been called down from New York to witness this. It was then that a colonel wearing the insignia of a U.S. Army Special Forces unit (it *may* have been the 10th Special Forces Group; time has clouded this detail) said that although Carol had demonstrated "high adaptability" to this novel warfighting training, within the past month, she had begun acting out violently very early in the pre-dawn morning hours towards her fellow soldiers in the barracks. One of the civilians, when Malachi asked *how* Carol had been acting out, replied that she had thrown several soldiers almost twice her size across the barracks, and when they hit the wall, they left an impression in it.

Malachi then asked to see the training materials, and he was presented with a set of thick binders that he began to page through carefully. After about twenty minutes of perusing the documents, Malachi looked at the assembled group and, in a very matter-of-fact tone without prevarication, told the assembled group that, in his opinion, Carol was suffering from demonic possession, and she needed a full, authorized exorcism. What's more, he told the assembled DoD personnel that they needed to immediately shut down this "training program," as he believed it actually *induced* Carol's state of demonic possession. I expected smirks and suppressed laughter from the small group around the conference table. Instead, several of the government attendees gave each other sideways glances and scribbled notes on the pads in front of them on the desk.

Later that afternoon, as the Amtrak Metroliner sped back towards Manhattan's Penn Station, I asked Malachi why he was certain that this involved demonic possession. Malachi said he saw that the alleged parapsychological "training materials" were created by Lieutenant Colonel Michael Aquino (since deceased). Malachi said that Aquino was a notorious Satanist who had specialized in psychological warfare development and operations for the U.S. Army since the Vietnam War. Aquino originally collaborated with the infamous California Satanist Anton LaVey but broke with LaVey over theological differences. Malachi told me that Aquino then founded a Satanic church known as the Temple of Set. He eventually came to the attention of Roman Catholic exorcists due to individuals who had been initiated into Aquino's Satanic Temple of Set and subsequently suffered from demonic possession. Given Aquino's fascination with psychological warfare, he was the author of a U.S. Army position paper, "From PSYOP to MindWar." The main thrust of "From PSYOP to MindWar" was as follows, taken from the Amazon book description of the similarly titled *MindWar* by Michael Aquino[5]:

---

1. CreateSpace Independent Publishing Platform; 2nd edition (July 4, 2016)

*MindWar proposes to eliminate war's killing and destruction by replacing it with a far more powerful kind of war—one that focuses on the human mind both individually and collectively. **The persons and property of people are removed as targets, replaced by the divisive situations and problems originating in their consciousness.** These are then controlled, adjusted, and reformed to produce a harmonious and cooperative total environment. **The price for this solution is that, for the first time in practical history, the actual machinery of human thought is accessed, by the methodical application of science, psychology, and esoteric arts of antiquity.** This book extrapolation and evolution of the original 1980 concept is not merely theoretical. It proposes "laboratory" implementation through the structural redesign of the U.S. Army's three "Special Operations" branches: Psychological Operations, Special Forces, and Civil Affairs.*

Malachi and another Roman Catholic priest subsequently performed the full Roman Rite of Exorcism as found in the Church's *Rituale Romanum* on Carol in the summer of 1991. The exorcism occurred under tightly controlled conditions at Fort Bragg's Womack Army Medical Center. Carol was eventually liberated from demonic possession, recovered from her trauma, and afterward became a well-respected artist living in Arizona.

Lt. Colonel Aquino could not have been pleased with this turn of events, although as his book *MindWar* amply demonstrated, he continued to advocate in his writings for using "science, psychology, and the *esoteric arts of antiquity*" for gaining a military edge in special operations warfare as late as 2013 after he retired from the U.S. Army. He subsequently authored a 2016 "50th Anniversary Edition" of Anton LaVey's *Satanic Bible* before he died in 2020.

14

TATI—HOW A CAIRN TERRIER
HUMANIZED A COLD SOUL

No account of my time with Malachi would be complete without an account of his beloved Cairn terrier, and for a fulsome description, I'd encourage people to read Malachi's book *A Priest and His Dog: The Tale of Tati*, published posthumously by Angelico Press. I first encountered Tati soon after meeting Malachi in 1990 at the Livanos household. When I first rang the doorbell of the Livanos' residence, I heard frantic barking and then a gentle admonition, "Shh, Tatis, it's only a visitor," but the little dog kept up its racket. Malachi opened the door, and when I entered, I saw a small white Cairn terrier reared back on its haunches, looking up at me like I was Goliath. I gave Malachi a curious look, and he told me Tati, whose name he pronounced as "Tatis," was harmless, was just overprotective of her master. He gently admonished her that I was a friend and to "mind her manners." In an instant, Tati went from the guard dog to a quietly obedient canine ball of love, dutifully trotting after her master and his guest to the kitchen.

We walked into the tiny kitchen (more of a food prep area) with a small Formica table and chairs. Little did I know I was about to make a fast friend. Tati diligently sniffed my pant leg, and I have no doubt she smelled the scent of my own dog at the time, a rust-colored cavalier spaniel rescue puppy named Harry. Malachi and I settled down to eat our sandwiches, and I soon realized I'd made the happy mistake of having a roast beef BLT. Tati quickly figured out I wasn't a threat but an *opportunity*. She smelled the rare roast beef, and before I realized it, she had gone from seeing me as a threat to seeing me as a "mark" for her loveable act as a doe-eyed con artist. The object of her desire was now apparent: a chunk of roast beef hanging from the end of my sub. I gave Malachi a curious look and asked if I could give her a little piece. Malachi grinned and said one small piece would be alright. Tati took the proffered scrap of roast beef dangling from my fingers with all the care of a surgeon's hands. Malachi told her, "Be a good girl, Tatis, and nap now; Rob and I have important things to discuss."

To my amusement, Tati gave a small, disappointed whine but obediently trotted to a small dog bed in the corner of the room, circled, and settled down with one protective eye fixed on Malachi. I couldn't help but marvel at how she seemed to understand him when he spoke. Although we were deeply discussing the recent Gulf War against Saddam Hussein, the topic soon turned to the little dog now gently snoring in her little bed. Malachi told me Tati was named for the daughter of Czar Nicholas and Alexandra, Grand Duchess Tatiana Romanov. Princess Tatiana was murdered in Yekaterinburg along with the rest of her family by Bolshevik Communist revolutionaries in 1918.

As time passed and my friendship with Malachi deepened, I realized the intense bond of affection that tied this little creature to Malachi and vice versa. When I encountered Tati, she was already almost eleven years old. She had been a fixture in the household since she was nearly a month old and barely weaned from her mother. Over time, Malachi slowly revealed how little Tati was a chosen instrument of Christ's love. He explained that his formal

Jesuit training had, over time, hardened a part of his soul into a place where no human emotions were permitted. This gradually introduced a certain priggishness into his personality that manifested with a distinct haughtiness. Malachi told me how he had taken pride in his intellectual prowess, and it manifested in his intellectual ability to, under almost any circumstance, cut a person down to size, leaving them shaken and humiliated. He told me how, over time, this pride threatened Malachi's relationship with the Lord Jesus. Malachi related to me that there had been times in Vatican City when he'd gotten into fiery debates with cardinals and archbishops, and his acid tongue had reduced them to trembling in terror.

I could see it pained him to admit this to me, and for my part, I must admit it was tough to imagine my genial, grandfatherly friend being a haughty verbal bully. Malachi told me that this haughtiness even manifested in his love of fencing, which was pretty much the only sport he indulged in. Whether with his épée or rapier, they were symbolic substitutes for Malachi's love of verbal jousting. This gradually introduced the poison of pride into his soul almost imperceptibly, and pride was the primary sin of the fallen seraphim Lucifer. But then the Lord Jesus saw fit to correct this malignancy in Malachi's heart, not with Ignatian prayer exercises, meditation before the Blessed Sacrament, or guidance from his spiritual director, but with a tiny, helpless Cairn terrier puppy. Slowly but inexorably, this little creature of God wormed her way into not just Malachi's life but the life of the entire household.

From when Tati was a tiny pup until she was about eight months old, it fell to Malachi to housetrain her. She was almost preternaturally intelligent in the precise meaning of the word. Tati spent much time on Malachi's little bed while he worked, either keeping careful watch over him or peacefully lying on her side sound asleep.

Malachi told me that as Tati matured into an adult dog, she could sense the presence of angels and demons and react accordingly. Malachi told me that in those times when the clamp of emotional loneliness wrapped its cold hand around his heart (as his priestly vow of celibacy still bound him), he truly began to take to Tati and her to him. He told me something about the relationship between humans and their animal companions that has colored my outlook to this day, whether it was with Harry, my late adopted cavalier spaniel, or one of our beloved cats. People view animal companions in one of two ways: either as a kind of "animal furniture," or they humanize their pets, thus making them a true part of their family.

With Tati, he would either pick her up so she was facing the crook of his elbow or, if she was on his bed, kneel by its side and softly talk to her while gently stroking her forehead. It wasn't the insensate, mushy baby talk many people use to communicate with their pets. Malachi would speak to Tati very simply but directly about many topics near to his heart. He would softly talk to her about his love of Our Lord and the Blessed Virgin, the Rosary, Saint Francis of Assisi, the angels, and God's love for all His creation, including little dogs like Tati. I don't think there was any off-limits topic, and I've no doubt Malachi confided his most intimate thoughts to his beloved little white canine. Through a singular act of God's grace, Tati somehow transcended her limitations as an "animal" (and how Malachi despised that word) and understood what Malachi was telling her. As he spoke to her about these things, a guttural moan would start in her trachea, and the more Malachi talked to her about these divine intimacies, the deeper and more prolonged her moans would become. It's difficult to describe, as it wasn't a dog's typical whining but akin to a soft groaning sound that grew deeper as Malachi softly whispered to her.

Malachi told me how, over time, little Tati effected a truly remarkable warmth in his heart. For a former Jesuit and a priest who didn't weep or stoically display any feelings at his mother's funeral or the deaths of his siblings, Tati slowly, in her spirited way, found the key to the stony "fortress he'd carefully built around his heart" to paraphrase the popular song by Sting. I only came to know Malachi after Tati had been a part of his life for ten years and didn't know him before Tati "softened his heart," as he put it. It's here that I must wade into the controversy of whether animals have either a "soul" or an element to their spirit that transcends the bonds of this mortal world. I will let Malachi express his feelings on this matter in his own words from his posthumous book *A Priest and His Dog: The Tale of Tati.*

"A small little dog, a terrier, a pedigree terrier, beautiful in her own way, with all the pedigree markings required by her breed— black tips to the ears and paws and tail, delicate snout, who never tired of being with me, who could be with me everywhere, who mirrored the joy of angels and their singular devotion, and above all a little dog who seemingly could transcend the obvious limitations of her canine nature. How could I not become dependent on her? This last point is tremendously important, that transcending power. There seems to have been definite phases in her life, especially in the last six years of her life, when she achieved self-reflective consciousness; when you could see clearly she was conscious of herself almost saying 'I am an I,' 'I am me, distinct from you.' There is a metaphysical and a supernatural question here."

Metaphysically, she never treated me as her master. She treated me as her father, her care-giver, her feeder, her charge. And in those special moments of her 'talking tours,' and, more par-

*ticularly during our 'moaning' sessions—I always called her 'mummy-puppy' plus a lot of other pet names—'lion in winter,' 'angel of God,' etc.—**there were intuitive moments when she was obviously straining against the bounds of her canine mortality, moaning and bemoaning, while my spirit kept assuring her that it was okay, that I had spoken to Our Lord Jesus, the Lord of Life and Love, that He would take her gently out of her mortality, that she would be with Him and with me forever.** And all this passed between us wordlessly with the arrow-straight silence of spirit entangling with spirit. I cannot tell you what that sweetness of soul, what that light in the mind, what that tenderness in the heart, were like. Only those who have experienced it will understand me."*

This begs the question: Do animals' spirits live on after their mortal death? I think Malachi's answer was obvious, given his passion for Tati, his transcendent bond with her, and the countless interactions I had with this remarkable little dog. They do not possess a *human* soul in God's image and likeness, but they have their own unique nature that transcends the icy grip of death, where their spirits are also embraced in the warm eternal light of Christ's love.

1 5

WHEN THE ANGELS SING

Malachi Martin not only had an immense love for the Lord Jesus, His Mother the Blessed Virgin Mary, and the saints, but he also had an extraordinarily deep relationship with the angels. Before a formal consecration event in 1991 that I was privileged to attend, I really had no idea how deep this relationship went or how profoundly it impelled different aspects of Malachi Martin's life. If I don't record what occurred at Paramus in July of that year, many details of exterior events and interior experiences will probably be forgotten. Back then I was still in the process of getting to know Malachi better as both a friend and spiritual director when he asked me to drive him to a discreet ceremony that was going to be conducted in a makeshift chapel tucked away inside the old Bergen Mall Shopping Center.

He told me that the ceremony was intended to deepen and formalize his relationship with the angelic realm of existence in the context of traditional Roman Catholic spirituality. When I asked him why this was necessary, given his already formidable theological depth as a former Jesuit, Malachi was already in the beginning phases of performing research and outlining the follow-up to his critically acclaimed nonfiction book published the year before *The Keys of This Blood*: *The Struggle for World Dominion Between Pope John*

Paul II, Mikhail Gorbachev and the Capitalist West. He told me that his next book was going to be another "factional" novel again, using the details and circumstances Malachi laid out in *Keys of This Blood* to tell the true story about the behind-the-scenes maneuvering by heretical and apostate senior Vatican clerics to get Pope John Paul II to resign the papacy and leadership of the worldwide Roman Catholic Church. He said that ever since the Pope's enemies inside the Vatican found out that John Paul II had Parkinson's disease, they sensed "blood in the water" and began actively plotting the removal of this pope from the governance of the universal Church.

In tackling his next book project involving Malachi's preoccupation with the critical issue of papal succession and, by extension, the universalism of Roman Catholicism, his involvement with the angels necessarily took a concrete step forward. This book, which would eventually become the bestselling hit *Windswept House*, would deal with the same basic subject matter that was the substance of his book *The Keys of This Blood*. As he performed the initial research for and then started to write *Windswept House*, it became apparent to him the fundamental issue was not *one* nation, society, or issue; it was the entire *society of nations*. He said that any intellectually honest observer would have a paradigm shift treading on this geo-strategic terrain involving mankind as a singular unit. Malachi quickly realized he had gone from considering the particulars of human beings segmented into neat little categories, such as religions, political ideologies, and nation-states, to dealing with the *entire human race as a family*. This naturally meant that he was now operating on the intellectual plane of dealing with God's universal lordship and governance of His created universe.

He said that in this paradigm shift, you go from the geopolitics of *reason* to the geopolitics of transcendent *faith*. Jesus saved us as *the human family* and as one unit (just as we were burdened with

Original Sin as a family, even though we will be judged finally as individuals). Catholic theology holds that although we were all saved as one family, considering salvation via Christ's Passion, Death, and Resurrection was made possible for all of us, in reality, not all of us will *de facto* be saved, only the Elect (due to individual life decisions made with our free will).

The overarching theme of what would eventually become *Windswept House* was papal succession, and the entire future disposition of the worldwide Roman Catholic Church after John Paul II had gone to his eternal reward was dominated by a controversial, malignant event that started the internal demolition of the institutional Roman Church organization in the early 1960s. Malachi confided this was a formal "enthronement" of Lucifer at the center of the Vatican institutional organization in a Satanic ceremony performed inside the Vatican's Pauline Chapel on the night of June 30–July 1, 1963. Malachi said if he were to expose this dire event publicly, he would be pulling back the curtains on the Kingdom of Darkness and its traitorous human cooperators' plans for the final subversion of the Church. This would be ostensibly accomplished by the formal alignment of the institutional Roman Catholic Church with the secular globalist adherents of the "New World Order." He was adamant that writing meaningfully about the topic would be impossible without extra spiritual protection. Already, in the early 1990s, many American bishops, archbishops, and cardinals had separated themselves from the Catholic Church through either tolerating/advocating heresy or had straight out apostatized from the Faith. I think that it was this current situation that led him to originally write *Hostage to the Devil*, as many senior Catholic churchmen since the mid-seventies seemed almost embarrassed to admit to the existence of a Personal Evil known as the fallen seraphic angel

Lucifer. They preferred to now think of evil in terms of nonpersonal structural sins of "racism, sexism, economic inequality, etc."

For those who've read *The Keys of This Blood*, it's a well-known fact that Malachi believed, because of this Satanic ceremony held in the Vatican in 1963, a malign power he alternately referred to as the "Superforce" or the "antichurch" had indeed ensconced itself in the Vatican. He said there was no other way to explain with a straight face the wholesale collapse of the Roman Catholic Church in the years since the close of the Second Vatican Council in 1965 and the current day (circa 1991). Thousands of Catholic priests, whether diocesan or priests in orders like the Jesuits, either petitioned Rome to be released from their vows (in other words, laicized) or just flat-out abandoned their vocations. Similar percentages of Catholic nuns abandoned their vows as well. Mass attendance dropped precipitously, belief in the Real Presence of Jesus's Body, Blood, Soul, and Divinity in Holy Communion declined, and traditional Catholic devotions like the Rosary and the Stations of the Cross fell into desuetude. Indeed, even Pope John Paul II's predecessor, Pope Paul VI, openly expressed his concern about the rapid decay that ravaged the Catholic Church since the close of the Council. In a speech to the Lombard Seminary in Rome on December 7, 1968, Pope Paul famously lamented that the Catholic Church, rather than being vivified in the wake of the Second Vatican Council, instead seemed to be engaged in a process of "self-destruction." Almost four years later, on the ninth anniversary of his election to the papacy and coincidentally the infamous enthronement of Lucifer in the Vatican's Pauline Chapel, June 29, 1978, Pope Paul VI shocked the Catholic world when he wrote, regarding the worldwide wholesale collapse of Catholic devotional practices and foundational beliefs, *"We would say that through some mysterious crack—no, it's not mysterious; through some crack, the smoke of Satan has entered the Church of God."*

Realizing the formidable nature of what he would be up against if he exposed the machinations of the Luciferian Superforce to destroy the transcendent elements of Roman Catholicism from within, by traitorous senior clergy who secretly referred to themselves as "Servitors of the Prince" (Lucifer), he was adamant that it would be impossible to write meaningfully about that without extra spiritual protection. Not content with invoking the Lord Jesus, the Blessed Virgin Mary, and his favorite saints, Malachi went the extra step of "calling in the cavalry": those mysterious creatures of God called *angels*. Malachi was led first to the cultivation of the angelic realm in general, then his Guardian Angel, and finally the cultivation of his Day Angel.

I think a key factor in Malachi's decision to write *Windswept House* was the urging of his Guardian Angel to undertake the baptism of aborted babies. Their Guardian Angels continuously advocated for their tiny martyred souls before Jesus, and some alliance was established between Malachi and these Guardian Angels merely because of his efforts on behalf of what he called "those little unborn martyrs." Malachi Martin was an ardent opponent of abortion, calling it "Lucifer's Sacrament" and that between 1970 and 1991, according to the best information available to the Vatican, several hundred million babies had been aborted in this silent genocide.[6] In a rare flash of anger, Malachi said that abortion was the spiritual equivalent of modern man's taking God's precious gift of life itself and defiantly vomiting it back in His face. Thus was Malachi Martin convinced that the dire warnings of the Virgin Mary at Fatima, and repeated at Garabandal and Akita (*the Father will send a punishment to mankind worse than the Flood such that the survivors will envy*

---

1. (Author's note: according to the Guttmacher Institute and the World Health Organization (WHO), as of 2025, this number is likely over a billion).

the dead...) were gridded to a timetable that was already running full-tilt.

This angelically prompted inspiration of Malachi to baptize the souls of aborted babies had its roots in Malachi's devotion to his Guardian Angel. He told me every person's connection or relationship to his or her Guardian Angel is established the moment you are conceived, clinging as a zygote to your mother's womb. The relationship is there for every human who has ever existed, whether you know it or not, whether you ever activate it or not, and whether you like it or not. In Malachi's case, that preparation was accomplished quietly, without fanfare or knowing where it would ultimately lead.

As a preparatory step, Malachi took up the habit of reciting the Chaplet of Saint Michael the Archangel as his first prayer when he woke up and as a preparation for all his daily prayers. This chaplet is a series of devotional prayers said on beads, much like rosary beads; indeed, it's sometimes called the "Rosary of Saint Michael." Reciting the chaplet gradually seeped into all his other devotions— the Holy Rosary, when he said Mass, taking Holy Communion, advising a church leader about pastoral practices, and more, as well as his writing, spiritual consulting, and lecturing activities. Malachi's spiritual director then decided it was appropriate for him to undertake a more formalized relationship with the angels, a consecration or dedication to them, and there was in existence an obscure but papally approved organization, the *Opus Sanctorum Angelorum*, ready, willing, and able to further Malachi's aspirations to deepen his intimacy with the angels.

A papally approved institution since the mid-twentieth century, the *Opus Sanctorum Angelorum* (Work of the Holy Angels), traced back to the private spiritual experiences of its foundress, Gabriele Bitterlich (1896–1978), an Austrian laywoman. The *Opus*

Sanctorum Angelorum has the scope and purpose of promoting devotion to the angels as the divine agents to effect the unity between creation and God in the context of the universe redeemed by Jesus. Pope Pius XII entrusted the *Opus Sanctorum Angelorum* to the Fathers of the Holy Cross in 1958, and as recently as the late Pope Benedict XVI, the Congregation of the Doctrine of the Faith issued a circular letter on the *Opus Sanctorum Angelorum* dated October 2, 2010, and subsequently published in L'Osservatore Romano on November 24, 2010, p. 17. In this letter, the Congregation makes official the approval of the "Statutes of the *Opus Sanctorum Angelorum*" by the Congregation for Institutes of Consecrated Life and Societies of Apostolic Life and the approval of the "formula of a consecration to the Holy Angels for the *Opus Angelorum*" by the Congregation for the Doctrine of Faith.

God deliberately created the angels because of the Incarnation of His Son as a member of a human race that needed divine redemption. Angels were not created as an independent forethought of God, unrelated to humanity within a material universe. The ancient fall of Lucifer came about because of his prideful refusal to worship and serve a member of humanity in a muddy Bethlehem stable that reeked of animal dung, a tiny, newborn creature that *in being* was inferior to Lucifer's angelic being. "I will not serve!!!" became Lucifer's cry of rebellion and revolt. *To kneel in adoration before a mewling human baby?!?!* NO! Consequently, Lucifer fell faster from Heaven than a flash of lightning sweeps from east to west, Jesus said (Luke 10:18). Catholic teaching from the Book of the Apocalypse, 12:7-8 says, "*And there was a great battle in heaven:* **Michael and his angels fought with the dragon, and the dragon fought, and his angels: And they prevailed not**, *neither was their place found any more in heaven.*" Indeed, the etymology of the Hebrew name Michael is transliterated as "*mî kəmo 'ēl*" where these elements together form the phrase "Who is like God?" The name Michael is thus understood as a rhetorical retort to Lucifer's aspiration to be like God. Given that Satanic or Luciferian elements within the Roman Catholic Church were actively plotting its destruction, Malachi thought it more than appropriate to enlist the aid of Saint Michael the Archangel in his public literary war against the evil infesting the Church.

I want to return to that 1991 day in Paramus. The makeshift chapel for the *Opus Angelorum* was stuck away in the old Bergen Mall Shopping Center, and a more upscale shopping center has long since replaced it. Inside, Father Zachary Monet, a Carmelite priest, waited for us (the good Father Zachary passed away in 2013). The chapel was empty, except for the invisible angels and the Blessed Sacrament. What followed for Malachi and the small group of lucky Catholics who had diligently prepared for the consecration to their angels had the atmosphere and characteristics of an interview with the Blessed Virgin Mary, the angels, and most importantly, the Lord Jesus Himself.

It would help if we imagined the golden silence in that chapel illuminated by the two six-branched candlesticks placed on the altar and pouring silently over the gold braid of the altar cloths, the golden background behind the altar, and the gold-yellow stonework in the walls of the sanctuary. It was all golden. The color tinged our hands, faces, and clothes with a transparent color of the same hue. We must also recall Father Zachary, the priest delegated to administer the Consecration. Looking back now, I remember he was well over six feet tall, with an ordinary face, eyes balanced at the top of his nose, surrounded by a complexion tinged with the ravages of age and disease, thinning hair, and a warm smile.

Father put on a surplice, stole, and cope, took the Blessed Sacrament from the tabernacle, placed It in the monstrance, then, with Malachi's assistance, placed some incense in the already lit

charcoal in the thurible. We all knelt and sang the *O Salutaris Hostia*.
How sweet it was to chant those sacred words composed by Saint
Thomas Aquinas. I can't accurately recreate the grace-filled moments
of that chant with words. Malachi told me the Lord Jesus *was* there:
Body, Blood, Soul, and Divinity, and with Him, His Father, and His
Holy Spirit. I fervently believed that with all my being.

Then, the ceremony of Consecration properly took place.
Father Zachary placed a lighted candle in the right hands of those
to be consecrated. Together, they recited the consecration to their
Guardian Angels, each of them inserting their name at the proper
place (I have enclosed a copy of Malachi's Consecration in his
handwriting as an appendix to this book). Then Father recited the
Prayer of Acceptance of the Consecration by the Church, followed
by a little sermon.

I really shouldn't call it a sermon. Father Zachary stood sort
of sideways on the lowest step of the altar so that he could simultaneously face us and the monstrance containing the consecrated
Host. He held a small pamphlet (the Adjuration of Angels), and he
proceeded to chat, a conversation with Our Lord and Our Lady, his
own Angel and the angels in general, and all the angels and saints
of God's Heaven. I wholeheartedly believe the Queen of Heaven and
all those others *were present* with Our Lord Jesus. It is impossible
to remember exactly what Father Zachary said, either in whole or
part, except to say it was just like a conversation between him and
"them," those august citizens of Heaven, with us laymen admitted
as privileged listeners, to whom an occasional nod was given when
what he said was particularly applicable to us. It was over before we
realized it. Then Father Zachary had Malachi put a ceremonial veil
on him, and Malachi incensed the monstrance.

Malachi later recalled that while we were singing Saint Thomas
Aquinas's famous hymn *Tatum Ergo*, he couldn't prevent his mind

from being flooded with memories of singing that very same hymn in his far-off Irish childhood days in Saint Michael's Ballylongford parish church, County Kerry, where he was baptized in 1921. The same church where his family went to Mass on Sundays and feast days until he was about six or seven. Every time the priest went down from the tabernacle with the Host and ciborium in his hands to distribute Holy Communion to the people kneeling at the altar rail, the young Malachi always saw a golden, supernaturally luminescent glow surrounding the ciborium holding the consecrated Hosts. He never asked his parents about this brightly shining glow emanating from the ciborium; he presumed everyone present in the church saw it, which came from the Jesus the adults spoke of. For Malachi, Father Zachary's simple benediction became a total resumption of all those past years before the Second Vatican Council (before I was born in 1961), when believers were immersed in living Catholicism and moved effortlessly within the accepted intimacy of Catholic faith and belief here on Earth. Malachi said Heaven was already with us all daily under the guise of traditional Roman Catholicism's "intimacy with the divine." It was not saccharine but sweet as a God-allowed foretaste of the Blessed in Heaven, the Church Triumphant.

Malachi's final words to me about angels, to the best of my recollection, went as follows: "Rob, you and other believers are on trial these days and months, so this revelation to you of the angels and their importance in salvation may be valuable to you, to remind you that the sweetness of God's company and Heaven's conversation is available to us here on our earthly pilgrimage. And who but the Lord Jesus is powerful enough, loving enough, and intimate enough with us to provide us this sustenance for our lives' journey?"

The work of the *Opus Angelorum* continues to this day, and more information may be found on their website: www. opusangelorum.org/

1 6

MALACHI'S LAST CALL

It was a May afternoon in 1999 when Malachi called me and asked if I'd drive him up to the Wilton, Connecticut, home of Dr. Rama Coomaraswamy, MD, PhD, to participate in an evaluation of a child who was potentially suffering from demonic possession. Dr. Coomaraswamy, who passed away in 2006, was a renowned cardio-thoracic surgeon at the Albert Einstein College of Medicine for several decades after graduating from Harvard University. After heart issues later in life precluded further work as a surgeon, Rama re-trained in clinical psychiatry, which he also taught at the Albert Einstein College of Medicine. Originally from Ceylon (now Sri Lanka), and the son of famed Hindu philosopher and art historian Ananda Coomaraswamy, Rama was raised in the Hindu faith and later converted to traditionalist Roman Catholicism. In addition to being a physician, Dr. Coomaraswamy was an author and a Roman Catholic priest ordained by independent Catholic bishops of the Thuc line and Malachi Martin, who participated as an unofficial representative of the Vatican. While Coomaraswamy adopted the sedevacantist position (that there hasn't been a valid pope since the death of Pope Pius XII), and Malachi did *not* (as evidenced by his many references to the validity of Pope John Paul II in his interviews with Canadian journalist Bernard Janzen right up until he died in 1999), this did not prevent a bond of friendship and dedication from forming between the two intellectual giants. I became good friends with Dr. Coomaraswamy after Malachi passed away.

That May morning, when Malachi and I drove up to Connecticut, we stopped for a coffee at a rest stop on I-95. Before proceeding on to the Coomaraswamy residence, Malachi and I walked around the parking lot, where he heard my confession as we strolled between the lines of parked tractor trailers. He said it was important that I be in a state of grace when we arrived, as he wasn't sure what we'd encounter. Malachi and I agreed to drop him off at Dr. Coomaraswamy's house at 9 a.m. and return for him at 2 p.m. The family was driving in from the Chicago metro area and was slated to arrive at 10:30 a.m., and Dr. Coomaraswamy and Malachi would interview their five-year-old daughter for about two and a half hours. But just like the old truism that no battle plan survives first contact with the enemy, to Malachi's dismay, the family's arrival preceded ours by about fifteen minutes. I pulled my Jeep in behind their Chevy Blazer, and Malachi and I got out.

We were introduced to the child, whom I'll call Marie, and her parents. I must admit that, at first glance, there appeared to be nothing wrong with the little girl. That all changed very quickly when, after the initial formal introductions were made, little Marie precociously marched up to Malachi, looked up at him with a very out-of-place smirk, and said in a distinctly adult voice, "You think you can help her, Malachi Martin? She already belongs to the Kingdom...." It took a lot to rattle me, but *that* shook me, the sheer assertive evil of those two sentences, defiantly claiming authority, coming from the mouth of a little child. Malachi quietly told me to leave, and I didn't need any more prompting. I got into my Jeep and soon headed to a diner about four miles away.

I arrived back at the Coomaraswamy residence several hours later, and Murphy's Law was in full effect again. The family was saying their goodbyes just as I pulled up to bring Malachi back to Manhattan when they were supposed to have left at least an hour earlier. Little Marie was already strapped into the back seat of the Chevy Blazer, and she pushed the button to lower her window. I thought she would say a simple "goodbye" to Malachi, but what happened then made me feel simultaneously sad *and* nauseous. This little girl, who should have been in the flower of childhood's innocence, gave Malachi a leering grin and blew him a kiss that could only be described as *lascivious*. It would be an understatement to say it creeped me out, but Malachi took it in stride. If I had to put a description to it, I'd say it was almost like a hooker blowing a kiss to a john after a satisfying liaison. The fact that it was such a young child was the very definition of obscene. On our ride back to New York City, Malachi was uncharacteristically subdued. Other than a quick "Oh yes" when I asked if he thought this was a legitimate case of possession, a reflective silence marked our two-hour ride back. I somehow knew he wasn't in the mood for any conversation. This is only my opinion, but seeing such a young child so in thrall to the Evil Spirit shook him. As a postscript to this unnerving episode, Marie was subsequently the subject of a successful exorcism by the late Bishop Robert McKenna.

Six weeks later came the beginning of the end of my earthly friendship with Malachi, at least here among us mortals in the Church Militant, trapped on what Malachi eloquently called "this geophysical time grid." As Malachi and I had birthdays only separated by two days, his on July 23rd and mine two days later, we'd typically meet for a relaxing dinner at the Isle of Capri restaurant on Third Avenue. The D'Agostino family, who owns the establishment, had long since taken this Irishman to their hearts. I had left the CIA for the private sector about a year earlier and was between jobs, trying to determine my post-Agency life. I was living in our family beach house down on the Jersey Shore.

On the late morning of Friday, July 23rd, the day we were to meet for dinner, my phone rang just before noon. It was Malachi in a shaky voice.

"Rob, I won't be able to meet for dinner tonight; I've taken a bit of a tumble. Old Scratch was unhappy with our trip up to Connecticut a few weeks ago, and he kicked my feet out from under me...." I was later to find out that he'd literally had his feet kicked out from under him, and he struck his head on the corner of a hardwood table as he fell.

Before I could say anything, he continued in a woozy, detached tone as I heard a commotion on the other end of the phone and the angry voice of Mrs. Livanos telling Malachi to hang up the phone.

"Rob, Kakia called an ambulance, and they're here. We'll talk soon."

Although I didn't know it then, those were the last words I ever heard Malachi Martin say to me. He was taken to Lenox Hill Hospital, where he was admitted with a cerebral hemorrhage, a severe internal bleed in his brain. By the time Malachi reached Lenox Hill, he was unconscious and would remain that way until his death on the following Tuesday, July 27th. That Sunday, I drove up to Manhattan early in the morning and went to visit him, hoping I'd be admitted to his room in the intensive care unit. The nurse in his room asked if I was family, and I lied with a straight face, saying yes, I was family.

She left the room, and I proceeded to pray the Rosary for Malachi. I had tears streaming down my face as I recited the ancient prayers, begging Jesus, the Lord of Life whom Malachi faithfully served, to mercifully and gently take the soul of his servant home.

He lay there in the hospital bed, hooked up to several beeping machines, his breathing steady but seeming a bit labored. It killed me to see him there like that, my best friend with his easy smile and quick wit, lying there unconscious, helpless and dying. I finished saying the Rosary and several other traditional Catholic prayers for the dying. I then went over to stand at his bedside and looked down at him.

I choked out the first awkward words in a bad cliché.

"Malachi, you can run, but you can't hide. We both know where you're going, and I'm asking you for three favors, even now. First, when you meet the Lord Jesus, ask Him to grant me the grace to see you again in His kingdom. Plus, you know I need a job since I haven't found anything since leaving the government. Finally, you know I've been trying to figure out my state in life. Please ask Our Lord what He wants from me in life. I'm feeling aimless. Do I have a vocation as a priest? Does He want me to be married? All I'm asking for is a clear sign."

A few minutes later, the nurse returned and told me I had to leave as the doctor would be in shortly. I have no problem admitting I was a basket case all the way home. He died two days later, on July 27th, and was laid to rest shortly afterward at a Traditional Latin Requiem funeral Mass at St. Anthony of Padua Catholic Church in West Orange, New Jersey. He was buried at Gate of Heaven Cemetery in Westchester County, New York. My friend, the holy priest of Jesus Christ, had gone home to his Divine Master.

Two of my requests of Malachi were answered with unmistakable clarity within five years of his death. The first request to be granted, for gainful employment, was answered by the offer of a job with the American Express General Counsel's Office only a month after Malachi passed away. I spent the next decade working at American Express, and my career as an anti-money laundering/

financial crime prevention executive in the banking industry was set in stone for the next twenty years.

Then, my plea for clarity regarding my state in life was answered when I met the beautiful woman who would become my wife, Wendy. Not long after we began dating, she told me her favorite entertainer was Elvis Presley. On one of our excursions in the New York Metro area before his death, Malachi confided that his musical "guilty pleasure" was *Elvis Presley!* Elvis was the only American "pop" singer he was a fan of besides Frank Sinatra. I never would have figured Malachi Martin was an Elvis fan, and to my knowledge, none of the people I've encountered over the years who were his friends and acquaintances knew Malachi was an Elvis fan.

My final request to hug my surrogate grandfather, best friend, and spiritual director in the Kingdom of God has yet to be realized.

By God's mercy, I remain hopeful.

UNPUBLISHED POEM BY MALACHI MARTIN
(From his book of Mass Intentions)

These are my friends, all my Souls
Who were once in the body,
And whom Jesus called to enter the life of the Spirit.
But not to leave me alone.
Rather to be nearer to me,
More than ever they were before,
When in their human body.
For now, only a thin interface separates us.
It is not their doing. Only my mortality,
And my condition *in Via*. They are *in Termino*.
Teach me, my friends.
All my Souls,
You who once were like me,
How to be with you now,
In spite of that interface. And teach me
That the nearer I am to Jesus, the nearer I am to you all.
So that when the end of time comes for me,
And that interface dissolves,
You will come for me—With Jesus and Mary and John and
Apollinaris and Father
Ignatius,
And Mummy and Daddy and Little Jim And Cozzie and Willie
And all my babies I have baptized.

And I will see Whom I have hitherto believed.
And I will possess what I have hoped to possess.
And I will be one with the Love I have sought. As Consummata's Priest.
In Jesus. Forever.

Amen.

MALACHI'S PRAYER OF CONSECRATION
TO HIS GUARDIAN ANGEL

Holy Guardian Angel,
who have been given to me
from the beginning of my life
as my guardian and companion.

I, poor sinner, Malachi Martin, desire
to consecrate myself to you
before my Lord and GOD
my heavenly MOTHER MARY
and all the Angels and Saints.
I wish to unite myself
closely to you forever.

In this union, I promise always
to be loyal and obedient
to my GOD and Lord and
to our holy Mother the Church.

I promise always to acknowledge
MARY as my Mistress,
Queen and Mother and
to imitate her way of life.

I promise to acknowledge you
always as my holy guardian
and to promote
as much as lies in my power
the veneration of the holy Angels
as the protection and the help
which is given to us
in a very special way
in these days of spiritual combat
for the Kingdom of GOD.

I beg you, holy Angel of GOD
obtain for me a love so strong
that I may be inflamed by it,
a faith so firm
that I may never falter.

I beg you to assist me
against the assaults of the enemy.

I beg you for the grace
of MARY's humility
so that I may escape all dangers
and, guided by you,
may reach the gates of our
heavenly home. AMEN

RECEIVED:

Fr. Z. A. Monet, O.Carm.

✝ Malachi B. Martin

A SURVIVAL GUIDE FOR CHALLENGING TIMES: THE SPIRITUAL INSIGHTS OF REVEREND DOCTOR MALACHI MARTIN

INTRODUCTION: INTIMACY WITH THE DIVINE AND HOLDING FAST TO THE TRADITIONAL CATHOLIC FAITH DURING SPIRITUAL UPHEAVAL

Malachi Martin was my spiritual director for ten years, and the Catholic wisdom he imparted to me is the most precious gift I have ever received, the literal version of the "pearl of great price" Jesus spoke of in Matthew 13:45-46. It was Malachi who brought me back to the practice of, and belief in, traditional Roman Catholicism. He also reintroduced me to the uniquely Catholic concept of "intimacy with the divine". When I asked him what the difference was between what Protestants call "a personal relationship with Jesus" and intimacy with the divine, he explained it to me this way. He said we all have personal relationships with people we encounter in the course of our daily lives. For example, you develop a relationship with your barber, your mailman, or your doctors. In this context, there's a certain amorphous quality to the concept of "a personal relationship with Christ." Catholics take this profoundly deeper when they receive the Blessed Sacrament, as we are actually entering into a relational intimacy with the physical Body, Blood, Soul, and Divinity of the Lord Jesus.

I have found my day-to-day faith occasionally rocked due to the 2013 abdication of Pope Benedict XVI and the late Argentine

Cardinal Jorge Bergoglio's ascension to the Chair of St. Peter as Pope Francis. A multiplicity of scandals and *ad hoc* heterodox pronouncements have followed in the ensuing thirteen years (as of this writing), either stemming from papal pronouncements in documents such as 2016's *Amoris Laetitia*, which opened the door to Communion for civilly divorced and remarried Catholics, or 2021's *Traditionis custodes*, that many traditional Catholics saw as a heavy-handed attempt at crushing access to the Traditional Latin Mass. It would take an entire book (and authors such as Henry Sire have done precisely this) to chronicle every troubling act and pronouncement of the late Pope Francis' papacy. Pope Francis has now gone to his eternal judgement and succeeded by the first American pope, Leo XIV, the former Cardinal Robert Prevost, in the conclave of May 8, 2025.

I will not wade in detail into the controversy about the validity of Francis's election and whether or not it violated the norms for the election of a pope set down by Pope John Paul II in his 1996 Apostolic Constitution *Universi Dominici gregis*, most especially parts seventy-nine and eighty-one (even though the late Cardinal Godfried Daneels seemed to gleefully admit just that in 2015, when the first edition of his biography was published). For the alleged illicit planning and covert plotting that went into the election of Cardinal Bergoglio to the papacy in 2013, I would direct the reader to Julia Meloni's excellent 2021 book *The St. Gallen Mafia: Exposing the Secret Reformist Group Within the Church*. These are Modernist churchmen who have lost their Catholic faith, belief in supernatural transcendent reality, and any sense of intimacy with the divine. One of Malachi's most memorable quotes about the Modernist clergy and their loss of the traditional faith was, "The worst punishment God can inflict on a soul is loss of the authentic Catholic faith. In their hubris and confident embrace of heresy and Modernism, these clergy *do not realize* they have apostatized. Otherwise, they would sacrifice their lives to get their faith back!"

A comment from Malachi to me back in 1996 is sufficient to expose the absolute rot permeating the Roman Catholic Church and society at large: "Rob, imagine if a devout, believing Roman Catholic from the year 1700 were transported to our time. They would look at the collapsed Church and our hyper-sexualized society, unable to recognize the Catholicism that permeated their own daily lives. They would think paganism had triumphantly returned to conquer civilization, regardless of our modern technology."

As if to ensure I understood the gravity of this observation, Malachi Martin pointed me to the prophetic warnings given by the Virgin Mary in her Church-sanctioned apparitions La Salette, France in 1846 (Rome will lose the Faith and become the seat of the Antichrist...) and, as discussed earlier, Fatima, Portugal in 1917. At La Salette, the Virgin Mary warned that "The priests, ministers of my Son, the priests, by their wicked lives, by their irreverence and impiety in celebrating the holy mysteries, by their love of money, love of honors and pleasures, have become cesspools of impurity. Yes, the priests are asking vengeance, and vengeance is hanging over their heads. Woe to the priests and to those consecrated to God who by their infidelities and their evil lives are crucifying my Son anew! The sins of those consecrated by God cry to Heaven for vengeance, and now vengeance is at their door, because there is no one left to implore mercy and pardon for the people. There are no more generous souls; there is no one left worthy of offering the spotless Victim to the Eternal on behalf of the world."

As late as 1999, just before his death, he was adamant that the vast majority of the Roman Catholic clergy has fallen into just the sort of de facto, if not de jure, apostasy as foretold in these aforementioned appearances of the Virgin Mary. This parallels, to a certain degree, the writings of the seventeenth century Spanish Dominican priest, Father Thomas Malvenda, who, citing such Catholic theological luminaries as Francisco Ribera, St. Robert Bellamine, and Francisco Suarez summarized their thoughts in Chapter Four of his work, "Commentarii in Apocalysin beati Ioannis Apostoli ad sensum litteralem exactissimi" ("Commentaries on the Apocalypse of Blessed John the Apostle According to the Most Exact Literal Sense): "Rome shall apostatize from the faith, drive away the Vicar of Christ and return to its ancient paganism... Then the Church shall be scattered, driven into the wilderness, and shall be for a time, as it was in the beginning, invisible hidden in the catacombs, in dens, in mountains, in lurking places; for a time it shall be swept, as it were, from the face of the Earth."

Given that we know from both Church-approved theological sources and apparations of the Virgin that in our times there will be large-scale apostasy, I wanted to distill Malachi's spiritual advice to me over the years down to its essentials, and this supplement is the practical result. I have endeavored to keep it simple and straightforward. There are traditional priests and lay theologians who are much more articulate and knowledgeable than I am; I'm only seeking to transmit the practical advice Malachi Martin gave me as my spiritual director. This short appendix is meant to help address the logical question people would ask if he were still living among us, "Malachi, if we are living in times of apostasy, what is the average Catholic believer to do...?" In times of turmoil, when the Church has appeared to be abandoned by Her shepherds, with the precedent set as described by the famous words of English martyr and bishop Saint John Fisher during the Protestant Revolt of the sixteenth century: "The fort is betrayed even of them that should have defended it. *And therefore, seeing the matter is thus begun and so faintly resisted on our parts, I fear we be not the men that shall see the end of the misery.*" In the face of priests, bishops, and cardinals who resemble wolves more than pastors, we must remember the Lord Jesus Christ's promises about His Mystical Body the Church: *"Behold I am with you all days, even to the consummation of the world"* (Matthew 28:20) and again when Christ said, *"And I say to thee: That thou art Peter; and upon this rock I will build my church, and the gates of hell shall not prevail against it"* (Matthew 16:18). The Church, as the Mystical Body of Christ, cannot fail; it is indefectible, but its human members are frail and often falter. When access to valid sacraments, valid Masses...and more becomes challenging, as noted in the chapter of this book entitled "Mass Confusion," or trust in the clergy is violated, it is not time for despair but to deepen our trust in Our Blessed Lord, His promises to us, the unfailing protection of His Mother the Blessed Virgin Mary, the saints, and the angels. This is especially true given the ambiguity surrounding modern Roman Catholic liturgical practice dating back to the post-Vatican Two pontificates of Popes Paul VI and John Paul II . The 'new' vernacular English language *Novus Ordo* Mass lends itself to *ad hoc* experimentation where observance of the Vatican's General Instruction of the Roman Missal (GIRM) are observed more often in the breach than practice. In the wake of the the late Pope Francis' 2021 Apostolic Letter *Traditionis custodes* severely restricting the Traditional Latin Mass, well-meaning Roman Catholics spiritually formed in the Traditional Latin Mass often find themselves thrust into irreverent, *'anything goes'* vernacular *Novus Ordo* Masses. These Roman Catholics, when faced with a dismissive "get-with-the-program" attitude from Church authorities more concerned with power than pastoral solicitude, **can't participate** because it involves willfully violating their conscience formed in centuries-old Catholic doctrine and practice.

The compulsion to embrace spiritual dissonance may constitute a **moral injury,** particularly if the experience is accompanied by profound mental conflict, guilt, or a sense of betrayal. Moral injury can be induced by being compelled to participate in a Mass with contemporary guitar or pop music, being socially pressured into kissing and hugging strangers at the Sign of Peace, jokes from the pulpit, informally dressed lay people casually distributing the Eucharist, and an overall atmosphere redolent of a social gathering more than a sacred sacrifice.

This is especially true when Catholics are powerless to change their situation, their beliefs and practices dating from antiquity are mocked or dismissed by Church authorities, and they subsequently face traumatic psychological conflict between obedience and conscience. Malachi Martin foresaw all of this over thirty years ago, and thus his admonitions to me at that time about the necessity of the 'underground Church.'

THE CRISIS FORETOLD: WARNINGS FROM HEAVEN

Any Catholic who knows their faith with a degree of spiritual intimacy and a sense of historical perspective knows that the Blessed Virgin Mary's apparitions at LaSalette, Fatima, Garabandal, and Akita were not merely dire warnings but the loving interventions of a concerned, caring mother. She came to us, foreseeing the spiritual dangers we would face and providing the tools to navigate them. LaSalette's prophecy that "Rome will lose the faith and become the seat of Antichrist" can seem overwhelming, but it also emphasizes our individual responsibility for the Faith. Similarly, in her 1917 appearances at Fatima, Our Lady's insistence on daily recitation of the Holy Rosary, consecration to her Immaculate Heart, and acts of reparation highlight that the solution, especially for us and our families, lies within our grasp.

Practical advice:

✢ **Daily Rosary:** Commit to praying all fifteen or at least one set of five mysteries each day, reflecting on key moments in the life of Christ as seen through Mary's eyes. Malachi, who daily said the entire fifteen-decade Rosary and Chaplet of Saint Michael the Archangel, would tell us to meditate on the particular scene of each mystery and place ourselves there spiritually, whether Our Lord's Agony in the Garden or the Assumption of the Blessed Virgin Mary into Heaven. Malachi told me many times to dedicate, if not all Five Sorrowful Mysteries, at least the Fourth Sorrowful Mystery, where Christ Carries the Cross to Calvary, to the most forgotten souls in Purgatory. He said, as Saint Padre Pio did, that these souls would become our advocates during spiritual trials and again when we appear before the judgment throne of Christ on our death.

✢ **Penance and Fasting:** Incorporate regular fasting into your spiritual life, offering sacrifices for the conversion of sinners and reparation for sins committed against the Sacred Heart of Jesus and the Immaculate Heart of Mary. If this seems too daunting at first, then adopt the older Catholic mortification of abstaining from eating meat on Friday.

✢ **First Saturday Devotion:** Participate in this comprehensive devotion given to us by the Mother of God at Fatima, which includes Confession, Holy Communion, recitation of at least five decades of the Rosary, and consoling Our Lady's wounded heart by meditating on the mysteries of the Rosary for fifteen minutes.

This devotion is to be practiced on the first Saturday of five consecutive months.

Prayers:

✢ **Act of Reparation to the Immaculate Heart of Mary:**
"O Blessed Virgin, Mother of God, look down in mercy from Heaven, where thou art enthroned as Queen, upon me, a miserable sinner, thine unworthy servant. Although I know full well my own unworthiness, yet in order to atone for the offenses that are done to thee by impious and blasphemous tongues, from the depths of my heart I praise and extol thee as the purest, the fairest, the holiest creature of all God's handiwork. I bless thy holy name, I praise thine exalted privilege of being truly Mother of God, ever virgin, conceived without stain of sin, co-redemptrix of the human race. I bless the Eternal Father who chose thee in a special way for His daughter; I bless the Word Incarnate who took upon Himself our nature in thy bosom and so made thee His Mother; I bless the Holy Spirit who took thee as His bride. All honor, praise and thanksgiving to the ever-blessed Trinity, who predestined thee and loved thee so exceedingly from all eternity as to exalt thee above all creatures to the most sublime heights. O Virgin, holy and merciful, obtain for all who offend thee the grace of repentance, and graciously accept this poor act of homage from me thy servant, obtaining likewise for me from thy divine Son the pardon and remission of all my sins. Amen (followed by recitation of the 'Hail Mary' three times)."

✢ The Fatima Prayer added to the end of each decade of the Rosary: *"O my Jesus, forgive us our sins, save us from the fires of Hell. Lead all souls to Heaven, especially those most in need of Thy mercy...."*

THE UNDERGROUND CHURCH: A HIDDEN REFUGE

In his interviews with Bernard Janzen, Malachi often spoke of the "underground Church," necessary in a time when massive numbers of the clergy had apostatized from the Faith. He stressed the underground Church is *not* about secrecy, but about personal fidelity to the timeless truths of Roman Catholicism in prudent hiddenness. The underground Church requires that Catholics remain connected to the truth and their uniquely Catholic "intimacy with the divine," even in isolation or when external support seems compromised. This has happened before in the history of the Church. Early Christians found strength in small, faithful communities in the face of Roman imperial persecution or heresies such as Arianism. Malachi told me that Japanese Roman Catholics, the *Kakure Kirishitan*, (Hidden Christians), after the suppression and persecution of Christianity by the Tokugawa shogunate, were forced to adapt and practice their faith in hiding. Today's underground Church calls for families and lay groups to uphold the Faith, although the challenges are different.

Practical advice:

- **Catechesis at Home:** Study the Catechism of the Council of Trent or the pre-1962 Baltimore Catechism to ensure doctrinal clarity.

- **Family Prayer Time:** Pray together as a family each day, emphasizing unity and faith in God's providence. Remember the motto of the famous Father Peyton's Rosary Crusades: *"The family that prays together stays together."*

- **Support Networks:** Form small groups of faithful Catholics to share resources, pray together, and provide moral and spiritual support.

Prayers:

- ✤ Frequently make an act of Spiritual Communion: "*My Jesus, I believe that You are present in the Most Holy Sacrament. I love You above all things, and I desire to receive You into my soul. Since I cannot at this moment receive You sacramentally, come at least spiritually into my heart. I embrace You as if You were already there and unite myself wholly to You. Never permit me to be separated from You. Amen.*"

- ✤ Pray to the Holy Spirit for discernment.

THE SOCIETY OF SAINT PIUS X AND THE PRESERVATION OF TRADITION

Malachi often championed the SSPX (Society of Saint Pius X) and their efforts to keep the traditional Catholic faith and Tridentine Latin Mass alive, saying the SSPX was a critical part of the underground Church. When people asked him if it was permitted to attend SSPX chapels, considering frequent and often threatening condemnation(s) by diocesan clergy, Malachi said, concerning valid sacraments, "When you are wandering in the desert and come upon a spring of clean water, *you drink.*" The SSPX plays a vital role in keeping the flame of tradition alive during a time of liturgical confusion, and Malachi said the SSPX was the equivalent of a chicken bone in the throat of the Modernist Church "because they can't swallow it, and they can't cough it up." Archbishop Lefebvre's defense of the Tridentine Mass and traditional theology offers stable anchors for Catholics seeking continuity with the Church's perennial teachings. While prudence is needed in navigating the SSPX's unique position within the Church, their commitment to sacraments of unquestioned validity is invaluable.

Practical advice:

✛ **Attend the Traditional Latin Mass:** Seek out an SSPX chapel or other communities validly offering the Tridentine Mass. Again, as Malachi said regarding sacramental validity, "If you are wandering in the desert and come upon a spring of clean water, *you drink.*"

✛ **Learn the Faith:** Use the Catechism of the Council of Trent or the pre-Vatican II Baltimore Catechism to deepen your family's understanding of Catholic theology, the Church Fathers, and traditional liturgy.

✛ **Defend Tradition with Charity:** Share the treasures of tradition without falling into divisive or combative rhetoric. Antagonism in defending the Faith is not Christ-like.

SPIRITUAL WARFARE AND THE ROLE OF OUR GUARDIAN ANGELS

In times of spiritual crisis, the battle is not only physical or intellectual but deeply spiritual. Angels, especially our Guardian Angels, are our powerful allies in this fight. The *Opus Angelorum*[7] emphasizes cultivating a direct relationship with your Guardian Angel, who can guide, protect, and strengthen you.

Practical advice:

✛ **Daily Angelic Devotion:** Begin each day by asking your Guardian Angel for guidance and protection with the Angel of God prayer below.

---

1. "In Communion with the Holy Angels Cum Sanctis Angelis" (2022), Opus Sanctorum Angelorum, https://opusangelorum.org/.

- ✤ **Discernment through Prayer:** Pray for your Guardian Angel's help in discerning truth amid confusion.

- ✤ **Study Angelology:** Learn about the hierarchy of angels and their role in God's plan through the writings of Saint Thomas Aquinas or the *Opus Angelorum.*

Prayers:

- ✤ The "Angel of God" prayer to our own Guardian Angel, *"Angel of God, my guardian dear, by whom God's love commits thee here, ever this day, be at my side, to light, to guard, to rule and guide. Amen."*

- ✤ The Chaplet of St. Michael.[8] According to traditionalcatholicprayers.com, the Chaplet of St. Michael the Archangel (or the Rosary of the Angels) was given to Antónia d'Astónaco, a Portuguese Carmelite nun, in 1751 by St. Michael the Archangel with the promises listed below. It honors St. Michael and the nine Angelic Choirs (Seraphim, Cherubim, Thrones, Dominions, Principalities, Powers, Virtues, Archangels, and Angels) and was approved and indulgenced by Ven. Pope Pius IX[9] in 1851: "Whoever would practice this devotion in his honor (St. Michael) would have, when approaching the Holy Table, an escort of nine angels chosen from each of the nine Choirs. In addition, for the daily recital of these nine salutations, he promised his continual assistance and that all the holy angels during life and after death deliverance from Purgatory for

2.   Reid, Jonathon (2019), "Chaplet of St. Michael, the 'Rosary of Angels," Traditional Catholic Prayers, https://traditionalcatholicprayers.com/2019/09/28/chaplet-st-michael/.

3.   "Chaplet of Saint Michael" (2025), Wikipedia, https://en.wikipedia.org/wiki/Chaplet_of_Saint_Michael.

themselves and all their relations." St. Padre Pio also recommended the St. Michael Chaplet to all his spiritual children and those suffering from temptation. It can be prayed daily or at any time.

PRAYER AS THE LIFEBLOOD OF THE UNDERGROUND CHURCH

Malachi often said that after the Second Vatican Council, he was convinced that Christ had withdrawn sanctifying grace from the Church's visible administrative structures, with one of the greatest signs of this calamity being the avalanche of priestly sexual abuse cases that burst on the scene after his death in 1999. Lay Catholics were left living in a state of canonical emergency, *even if they didn't realize it*. Malachi also said that generations of Catholics had been led by their nose out of their Catholic faith into practical apostasy without even realizing it. This was the negative side of the ancient Catholic dictum *lex orandi, lex credenti* or the 'The law of prayer is the law of belief.' It highlights the close relationship between liturgical practice and theological belief in Catholic tradition. With the visible degradation and countless innovations in the post-1970 Mass, Catholics were led to believe that foundational elements of once bedrock elements of Roman Catholic belief were now somehow optional.

In such a dire time, prayer becomes the foundation of our spiritual lives if we are left without certain access to valid sacraments, especially Confession and reception of the Blessed Sacrament. The Rosary, the Chaplet of Saint Michael, and the Liturgy of the Hours provide a structure for anchoring ourselves daily in God. Malachi also strongly recommended meditating on Scripture because it allows us to hear God's voice even in silence.

Practical advice:

- ✝ **Set a Daily Prayer Schedule:** Create a consistent prayer routine, incorporating morning, midday, and evening prayers.

- ✝ **Pray as a Family:** The Rosary is especially powerful when prayed together, fostering unity and mutual support. Again, remember the motto of Father Peyton's Rosary Crusades: "The family that prays together stays together."

- ✝ **Make Frequent Acts of Spiritual Communion:** When the Eucharist is unavailable, make frequent spiritual communions to maintain union with Christ.

Prayers:

- ✝ The Holy Rosary and Chaplet of St. Michael the Archangel
- ✝ Liturgy of the Hours or abbreviated forms like Morning and Evening Prayer

LIVING VIRTUOUSLY: LESSONS FROM SAINT PADRE PIO

Malachi often invoked St. Padre Pio's intercession, encouraging devotion to him even before St. Pio's elevation to sainthood. Padre Pio's holiness was rooted in simplicity and obedience. As a living example of Jesus's sufferings through his patient bearing of the *stigmata*, the Wounds of Christ, he showed faithfulness to God, transforming trials into grace, even amid suffering. St. Padre Pio's emphasis on Confession, prayer, and trust in God offers a template for navigating a spiritual drought. It's instructive to remember often emphasized the importance of trust in God and inner peace through his famous saying: "Pray, hope, and don't worry. *Worry is useless.* God is merciful and will hear your prayer."

Practical advice:

- **Confession When Possible:** Seek regular, weekly confession when available, and make frequent acts of contrition when it is not.

- **Offer Your Suffering:** Unite your daily crosses with Christ's suffering on the Cross for the salvation of souls.

- **Cultivate Joy:** Despite trials, find joy in small blessings, trusting in God's providence.

Prayers:

- Act of Contrition: *"O my God, I am heartily sorry, I am heartily sorry for having offended Thee and I detest all my sins, because I dread the loss of Heaven and the eternal fiery punishments of Hell, but also because I have offended Thee, my God, who art all good and deserving of all my love. I firmly resolve, with the help of Thy grace, to confess my sins, do my penance, and amend my life. Amen."*

- Prayer of St. Pio of Pietrelcina after Holy Communion (which can be recited after making a spiritual communion in the event access to the Blessed Sacrament isn't available):

  Stay with me, Lord, for it is necessary to have You present so that I do not forget You. You know how easily I abandon You.

  Stay with me, Lord, because I am weak and I need Your strength, that I may not fall so often.

  Stay with me, Lord, for You are my life, and without You, I am without fervor.

Stay with me, Lord, for You are my light, and without You, I am in darkness.

Stay with me, Lord, to show me Your will.

Stay with me, Lord, so that I hear Your voice and follow You.

Stay with me, Lord, for I desire to love You very much, and always be in Your company.

Stay with me, Lord, if You wish me to be faithful to You.

Stay with me, Lord, for as poor as my soul is,

I want it to be a place of consolation for You, a nest of love.

Stay with me, Jesus, for it is getting late, the day is coming to a close, and life passes; death, judgment, and eternity approach. It is necessary to renew my strength, so that I will not stop along the way, and for that, I need You.

It is getting late, and death approaches,

I fear the darkness, the temptations, the dryness, the cross, the sorrows.

O, how I need You, my Jesus, in this night of exile!

Stay with me tonight, Jesus, in life with all its dangers. I need You.

Let me recognize You as Your disciples did at the breaking of the bread, so that the Eucharistic Communion be the Light which disperses the darkness, the force which sustains me, the unique joy of my heart.

Stay with me, Lord, because at the hour of my death, I want to remain united to You, if not by communion, at least by grace and love.

Stay with me, Jesus, I do not ask for divine consolation, because I do not merit it, but the gift of Your Presence, oh yes, I ask this of You!

Stay with me, Lord, for it is You alone I look for, Your Love, Your Grace, Your Will, Your Heart, Your Spirit, because I love You and ask no other reward but to love You more and more.

With a firm love, I will love You with all my heart while on earth and continue to love You perfectly during all eternity. Amen."

PREPARING FOR THE WARNING AND THE TRIUMPH OF THE IMMACULATE HEART

Malachi Martin personally knew Conchita Gonzalez Keena, one of the seers of the as-yet unapproved apparitions of Our Lady at Garabandal, Spain, in the early 1960s, and he arranged for me to meet her personally at her home in Queens, New York, in 1996. I remember Conchita as gracious, somewhat shy, and deeply devoted to Our Lord and Our Lady. The Warning, or the worldwide illumination of conscience, foretold at Garabandal by Our Lady (and prophesied by saints and Church mystics as well) will illuminate every soul's spiritual state before God, offering a profound opportunity for repentance. By living life in a state of sanctifying grace, we can prepare our souls for this moment and contribute to the triumph of the Immaculate Heart of Mary as foretold by Our Lady of Fatima.

Practical advice:

✦ **Frequent Examination of Conscience:** Spend time daily reflecting on your sins and weaknesses. Afterward, recite a sincere "Act of Contrition" prayer.

- **Practice Devotion to** Mary: Consecrate yourself to the Immaculate Heart, ideally through the formal *Consecration to Jesus Through Mary* by St. Louis de Monfort and pray for her intercession.

- **Live with Your Eternal Destiny in Mind:** Make decisions that align with God's will, always prioritizing your eternal soul.

Prayers:

- Malachi advocated Consecration to the Immaculate Heart of Mary using Father Faber's translation of St. Louis de Monfort's *True Devotion to Mary: With Preparation for Total Consecration* (available from Amazon.com and many online Catholic booksellers).

- Act of Hope: *"O my God, trusting in Your infinite goodness and promises, I hope to obtain pardon of my sins, the help of Your grace, and life everlasting, through the merits of Jesus Christ, my Lord and Redeemer. Amen."*

RESOURCES

The Catholic Company is an excellent and reliable source for traditional Roman Catholic prayer compilations, like the 1958 *Raccolta* collection of official Catholic prayers and devotions issued under the authority of Pope Pius XII, and sundry items such as Traditional Latin Mass missals, holy medals, scapulars, and rosaries.[10]

---

4. "The Catholic Company," (2025), https://www.catholiccompany.com/.

ACKNOWLEDGMENTS

I wish to gratefully acknowledge the assistance and insights of Father Charles Murr, Dr. and Mrs. Anthony Stine, Kennedy Hall, and Joe McLane in writing this book. My fellow Catholics, I owe you a profound debt for your collective contributions.

I would also be remiss if I did not acknowledge the critical input of Rachel Mastrogiacomo, a brave clerical abuse survivor. Her story serves as proof that Malachi Martin's warning that satanic infiltration in the Roman Catholic Church continues to the present and is dismissed at our peril.